ANNIKET COLEMAN'S

Lady Golfers Guide

BUYING USED GOLF CLUBS	52
CARE & MAINTENANCE OF CLUBS	**54**
WHAT TO LOOK FOR IN GOLF SHOES	**55**
BASIC RULES OF THE GAME	**57**
GOLF HOW TO'S	**65**
How to mark a Scorecard	65
How to Use a Ball Washer	67
How to Repair a Divot	68
How to Rake Sand Bunkers	69
How to Clean Your Golf Clubs	71
How to Clean Your Golf Club Grips	73
50 GOLF TIPS FOR LADY GOLFERS	**75**
GOLF LESSONS	**89**
Lesson 1: Six Habits That Will Help Your Handicap	89
Lesson 2: How to Develop the Perfect Pre-Shot Routine	90
Lesson 3: Five Steps to Develop the Perfect Putt	92
Lesson 4: Mastering the Second Most Important Club in Your Bag	93
Lesson 5: Four Tips for Playing Golf in a Gale	94
Lesson 6: Finding the Fairway	95
Lesson 7: Many Players are Afraid of the Right Side. Don't Be!	97
Lesson 8: How to Turn Bunker Play into a Day at the Beach	98
Lesson 9: Our 6 Best Tips for Hitting From the Rough & Other Tough Lies	99
Lesson 10: Our Best Tips for Hitting out Of a Side Hill Lie	101
Lesson 11: How to Be At Your Best in the Rain & the Cold	102
Lesson 12: Our Five Best Tips to Help You Hit Woods with Confidence	103
Lesson 13: Know Your Faults & How to Fix Them	105
Lesson 14: 5 Ways to 10 More Yards	107
Lesson 15: Learning To Manage Your Game	108
Lesson 16: Learn Seven Drills to Putt Consistently	110
Lesson 17: Our Six Ways to Eliminate Your Slice	112
Lesson 18: Playing From Various Bunker Lies	114
Lesson 19: Learning to Properly Release the Club	115
Lesson 20: Learn To Transfer Your Weight	118
Lesson 21: Learn to Check Your Alignment	120
Lesson 22: Adopting Proper Putting Fundamentals	121
Lesson 23: Getting Your Total Game in Shape	123
Lesson 24: Getting Out Of Trouble Spots	125
Lesson 25: The Art of the Bump & Run	126
BAD SHOTS IN GOLF	**129**

MORE SHORT GAME TIPS — 133

Pitching — 133
Chipping — 134
Sand Play — 137
Putting — 138

SPECIALTY SHOTS - SHOT MAKING — 142

How to Hit a Fade — 142
How to Hit a Knockdown Shot — 144
How to Play to Low Shot — 144
How to Play a Lob Shot — 145
Hit Down to Go Up — 146
Playing in the Wind — 146

TROUBLESHOOTING — 149

Diagnosing the Push Shot — 149
Diagnosing the Pull Shot — 150
Diagnosing the Slice — 151
Diagnosing the Unwanted Fade — 152
Diagnosing & Curing the Hook — 153
Topping the Ball — 154
Casting — 154

COURSE MANAGEMENT — 156

How to Handle Awkward Lies — 156
How to Play the Par 3 — 159
Cold Weather Play — 160
Rough Play — 162
The 70 Per Cent Trick — 163

FITNESS TIPS FOR LADY GOLFERS — 165

HOW TO PREVENT GOLF INJURIES — 166

Weight Tips — 169
Eating to Loose Weight — 170
Golf and Pregnancy — 170
Tips for Stamina — 171

IMPROVE YOUR GOLF WITH YOGA FOR GOLFERS — 173

Why Yoga for Golfers? — 173

WHAT IS YOGA?	173
GETTING STARTED WITH YOGA FOR GOLFERS	174
YOGA EQUIPMENT	175
YOGA MEDITATION	176
CORRECT BREATHING IN YOGA	176
SEQUENCE OF POSES IN A YOGA SESSION	178
YOGA STANDING POSES	188

KIDS AND GOLF 196

WHEN TO GET THEM STARTED	196
HOW TO GET THEM STARTED	196
TAKE THEM TO THE COURSE	197

GOLF GLOSSARY 198

Women and Golf

Women's golf has seen an incredible rise in popularity over the past decade or so, and that popularity continues to grow. From the days when golf was the pastime of a selected group of 'upper class males' who walked the greens in their checkered pants, ladies on the golf course are now a common sight – and rightfully so.

The reasons for this development may be plentiful, but most of all women have realized that golf is a great way to work out not only their body but also stress and frustration. Of course, the latter two are a double edged sword – golf can make you even more stressed out and frustrated due to the nature of the game. Two games of golf are never the same, one day it may be the most fun while the next day it can be the most infuriating. This book will help you to shift the balance more towards the fun part.

With more and more female golfers hitting the links the golfing industry has adapted as well, most notably in developing a whole range of golf equipment, accessories and apparel especially for Lady Golfers. We will be looking at some of the developments that will help you in your game. After being in this industry for quite a while I will also share some 'wisdom' so that you don't fall blindly into any consumer trap.

However, before we go into the thick of things I need to tap on one major issue I've been seeing all over:

Golf Course Blues

Lady Golfers – the very real issue of being intimidated on the golf course, while serious, needs to be put behind us. Given that women are more flexible than men, have more efficient swings, and are more naturally suited to the game than our male counterparts one has to wonder why we are so intimidated by being on the course or by male golfers?

While the average male does have more upper body strength than the average female, pound for pound, women get the job done more efficiently and more consistently than our muscle-bound friends do. Given the extra weight (we'll try to be nice here) and strength of the male, you would think that they could out-hit us by a considerable margin – but they don't. Consider the petite five foot 2 inch, 90 pound, middle-aged Lady Golfer cracking the ball 150 yards. Then consider the 180-pound muscle bound 22-year-old. He sizes the ball up, leverages all of his strength and sends it 180 yards slicing down the fairway into the woods. Even if he hits it 200-220 yards, the effort required to generate the result is far greater than the efficient engine our Lady Golfer represents. Ladies, there is just no comparison.

Add to the fact that the Lady Golfer's drive will land fair and true in the centre of the fairway, while the muscle-bound guy will spray his shots uncontrollably through brush and into water and we should be working from a position of superiority, not intimidation.

Muscle does not make a good swing. Distance alone does not make a good golfer. Yet this, coupled with a certain arrogance by males on the golf course cause a very high level of intimidation even while our muscle-bound friend plays golf no better than we ourselves might.

So why does this happen and what can we do about it?

First, understand why you're out golfing. We're supposed to be out for a good time, to relax and to be with friends. To make sure you keep this at the forefront of your thoughts, golf with people, either women and/or men, who are like minded, and, like skilled.

Second, don't fall into the trap of thinking that distance is everything in golf. Consistency and finesse are the name of the game. The Grande Mama, Mary, Queen of Scots – golf's first monarch learned the secret - drive for show and putt for dough. Unfortunately, just after she learned this, she lost her head (more about this below). The number one objective off the tee is to get the ball in a good position for the next shot – not to be looking for the ball in the woods. Be patient, bide your time.

Third, if you find yourself in a foursome with a couple of arrogant males, don't get flustered by how they shoot – just play your own game. These are men who are completely engrossed in their own performance, such as it is, and are about as sensitive as a sack of horseshoes to everything around them. You'll never hear a compliment out of the mouth of this type of golfer so don't expect any after a good shot.

With this off my chest let's move on…

I believe it is good to have a wholesome understanding of the game, not only talk about the technical part alone. In this light let's take quick look at…

A brief History of Golf

A lot of controversy exists about how it all started. Roman emperors apparently played a relaxing game called 'paganica', using a bent stick to drive a soft, feather-stuffed ball. Over the next five centuries the game developed on several continents and eventually evolved into the popular Scottish game known as 'golfe'. Various European countries had games resembling paganica – 'cambuca' in England, 'jeu de mail' in France, and in the Netherlands 'het kolven', which was played in the American colonies as early as 1657.

The origin of golf differs throughout the world. Most countries associate the sport with sticks and balls with no mention of a rabbit hole. Regardless of the claims, the Scots indisputably popularized the game.

In 1754, the St Andrews Society of Golfers was formed and golf was recognized as a sport. In 1764, an 18-hole course was constructed and St Andrews became the standard for all others to emulate. In 1854, the famous clubhouse was erected. Thereafter, the Royal and Ancient Golf Club of St Andrews (R&A) became the flag-bearer of the game as a sport.

Golf is a woman's game as much as it is a man's. Women have been involved in the game pretty much since its inception in the 13th century. The game has had its ups and downs over those years. The year 1587 was a down year for women's golf with Mary, Queen of Scots, and golf's first famous woman player, being convicted of treason and beheaded. That was a pity – her short game was just starting to come around... Needless to say, this kept more than a few women from learning to play and could be the reason why so many women today feel intimidated by the game.

Women's golf did finally come around again. In 1810 the first women's tournament was held for Scottish fishwives in Musselburgh (quite appropriately named I think). Then in 1893, the first women's golf championship, organized by the Ladies Golf Union in England was held. The women's game has never looked back.

In 1820, the first golf club outside Britain called the Bangalore appeared in India. Clubs in other countries such as Ireland, France, Australia, Canada, South Africa, USA and Hong Kong began to make an appearance in the 19th century. The St Andrews of New York was the club that started the craze in the US.

early 'Longnose' Golf Clubs

In the olden days a golf club was made entirely of wood and resembled the shape of a hockey stick. Clubheads were originally made from holly, beech and pear. Shafts were constructed of ash or hazel. The head was secured to the shaft using a splint wound with leather straps. Clubs were costly because of the painstaking labor involved. Moreover, these clubs weren't durable; golfers would often break 1 or 2 clubs during a single round. Thus, the game wasn't affordable for common folks.

Balls consisted of compressed feathers wrapped with leather. Called the "featherie", this ball was laboriously made by hand. Due to the high cost of this handcrafted equipment, the game wasn't available to ordinary citizens.

Featherie Golf Ball

In 1848, Rev. Adam Paterson invented the 'Guttie' – a more durable ball made of gutta-percha which eventually replaced the expensive 'featherie' ball. The 'guttie' proved too much for the longnoses. To cope with the higher stress of this ball, manufacturers used additional wood to reinforce the clubhead. These clubs or 'bulgers' had bulbous heads and resembled modern day woods.

Guttie Golf Ball

The durable Guttie gave rise to the creation of clubs with iron heads. These clubs were aptly called irons. Although they could perform high rising shots, they couldn't out-distance shots by wooden clubheads. These longer-hitting 'woods' retained their wooden clubheads with persimmon as the choice material.

In the 1920s, the first steel-shafted clubs began to appear in the US. In 1931, Billy Burke was the first person to win the US Open with steel shaft clubs. At this time, the sand wedge was being developed.

In 1939, the R&A imposed a limit of 14 clubs that a golfer could use in tournaments. Clubs were also assigned numbers instead of names. Woods were numbered one through five, and irons two through nine. The putter retained its name instead of being assigned a number.

In 1963, mass production of clubheads was made possible by casting. This lowered the price of clubs. However, professionals still preferred hand-forged clubs because of their superior 'feel' and control. Mass production made the game affordable to the average person and contributed to the phenomenal growth of the sport.

In 1973, the graphite shaft was introduced. Graphite was lighter, stronger and more rigid than steel. Modern graphite shafts included a matrix or other materials for better performance. Currently, many golfers use steel shafts because they're cheaper. Most professionals use steel shafts because they are easier to control.

The most successful club in history is the Big Bertha manufactured by Callaway in 1991. This club has an oversized persimmon wooden clubhead. Taylor-Made became the first company to manufacture metal woods. The current trend is woods with titanium heads that are fitted with graphite shafts.

1991 'original' Big Bertha

Among the major men's tournaments are the Masters, the U.S. Open, the British Open, and the PGA. Women golfers have their own tour, sponsored by the Ladies Professional Golf Association (LPGA), the governing body for about 600 women professionals.

Women's golf does not have a globally agreed set of majors. The LPGA's list of majors has changed several times over the years, with the last change in 2001. Like the PGA TOUR, the LPGA currently has four majors:

Kraft Nabisco Championship
U.S. Women's Open
LPGA Championship
Women's British Open

As in men's golf, three of the majors are played in the United States and one is played in the United Kingdom. The U.S. and British Opens match their male equivalents, and the LPGA Championship is analogous to the PGA Championship, so by default the Kraft Nabisco Championship is the closest equivalent of The Masters. Unlike the men's equivalents, with the sole exception of the U.S. Women's Open, the women's majors have title sponsors.

Golf is played, to some extent, in most countries of the world. In Japan, for instance, golf is sometimes regarded as the national pastime. The Ryder Cup, which begun in 1927, is a biennial men's professional competition that used to be between a U.S. team and one representing England, Scotland, and Ireland. In 1979 the latter team was expanded to include members from all of Europe. The Walker Cup and Curtis Cup are amateur competitions for men and women respectively, between teams from the United States and England, Scotland, and Ireland. The former began in 1922 and since 1947 has taken place in odd-numbered years. Curtis Cup competition began in 1932 and is held in even-numbered years.

Outstanding Female Golfers

Joyce Wethered

She was born on Nov. 17, 1901, in Devon, England and died on Nov. 18, 1997. Joyce 'Wethered' was her maiden name, she was later better know as by her married name, Lady Heathcoat-Amory.
Joyce Wethered dominated women's golf in Britain in the 1920s, at the same time Glenna Collett Vare was dominating American golf. The two only met on the golf course three times, and Wethered won all three matches. At age 19 she won the 1920 English Women's Amateur title, and subsequently the next four as well, going 33-0 in match play. Her first victory in the British Women's Amateur came in 1922, and she followed up with wins in '24 and '25. One of the most famous male golfers on that time, Bobby Jones, once remarked after a casual game with her: "I have not played golf with anyone, man or woman, amateur or professional, who made me feel so utterly outclassed."

Glenna Collett Vare

Born on June 20, 1903, in New Haven, Conn., she was know as the 'Queen of American Golf'. Most notably she won the U.S. Women's Amateur: 1922, 1925, 1928, 1929, 1930, and 1935. Vare also won two Canadian Women's Amateurs and one French Women's Amateur, but never the British Women's Amateur, where she twice lost to nemesis Joyce Wethered (see above). Possibly her Perhaps her best year was 1924, when Collett Vare won 59 of 60 matches played. In honor of her name the golfer with the lowest scoring average on the LPGA Tour each year has received the Vare Trophy (since 1953), while the winner of the U.S. Junior Girls Championship is awarded the Glenna Collett Vare Trophy. She was inducted into the Golf Hall of Fame and died Feb. 3, 1989.

Mildred 'Babe' Didrikson Zaharias

Born in 1914, Mildred 'Babe' Didrikson Zaharias (right) was the most notable post-war female golfer. She is undoubtedly one of the greats in the history of women's golf. But a strong argument can also be made that Babe Didrikson Zaharias was the greatest female athlete of all-time. Writing about her in 1939, *Time* magazine described Babe as a "famed woman athlete, 1932 Olympic Games track & field star, expert basketball player, golfer, javelin thrower, hurdler, high jumper, swimmer, baseball pitcher, football halfback, billiardist, tumbler, boxer, wrestler, fencer, weight lifter, adagio dancer." During the 1932 Olympic tryouts, she won 5 of the 8 track and field events she entered and she broke 4 world records in the process! This extraordinary woman won the US Women's Amateur in 1946, the Women's British Amateur in 1947 and the US Women's Open in 1948, 1950 and 1954.

Nancy Lopez

Nancy Lopez won 48 Tour victories and 3 Majors from 1978 to 2003, despite having given birth to three children during this time. Born Jan. 6, 1957, in Torrance, California, she was introduced to golf by her father when she was eight. Just four years later she won the New Mexico Women's Amateur at age 12, and the U.S. Junior Girls Amateur in 1972 and '74. She turned pro in 1977 and joined the LPGA the following year. In her first year with the LPGA she won an amazing nine titles, including five in a row. In 1985, just after the birth of her first child, she won the money title, the scoring title and the Player of the Year Award. She set up a company, Nancy Lopez Golf, which produces a full line of women's clubs and accessories.

Annika Sorenstam

Born Oct. 9, 1970, in Stockholm (Sweden), she took up golf at the age of 12. Sorenstam turned pro in 1993 and was Rookie of the Year on the Ladies European Tour. That first LPGA win finally came at the 1995 U.S. Women's Open, and Sorenstam took off on what might be the best career in LPGA history. From 1995 through 2006, Sorenstam won eight money titles and never finished lower than fourth. She won 69 tournaments and 10 majors in that span. She is clearly one of the best female golfers ever. Ely Callaway: "In my life in golf, she hits it dead solid more consistently than any golfer I've ever seen."

Anatomy of a Golf Course

The simple objective of this game is to hit a small spherical object called a golf ball into a hole using a piece of equipment called a golf club.

Technically, all you need is one golf club and one golf ball. You can perform this task with one stroke or one hundred strokes. Of course, your goal is to sink the ball with as few strokes as possible. That is where the difficulty lies.

As we said earlier, golf is played by holes. It should be noted that "hole" can mean either the actual hole in the ground into which the ball is played, or the whole area from the teeing ground (an area of specially prepared grass from where a ball is first hit) to the putting green (the area around the actual hole in the ground). Most golf courses consist of 9 or 18 holes. (The "19th hole" is the colloquial term for the bar at a club house.) For the shortest holes a good player requires only one stroke to hit the ball to the green. On longer holes the green is too far away to reach it with the first stroke, so that one or more strokes are played from the fairway (where the grass is cut so low that most balls can be easily played) or from the rough (uncut grass or ground not prepared at all).

Many holes include hazards, namely bunkers (also called sand traps), from which the ball is more difficult to play than from grass, and water hazards (lakes, ponds, rivers, etc). Special rules apply to playing balls that come to rest in a hazard which make it highly undesirable to play a ball into one.

Let's look at some of the components of a golf course in a bit more detail:

Tee Sign/Layout

As you walk to the first hole, you will notice a tee sign, a board telling you all about the current hole.

The picture on the right shows a tee sign. It usually includes a diagram of the shape of fairway leading to the green with hazards marked along the way. The first row always indicates the number of the hole. In this case, the layout shows HOLE 1.

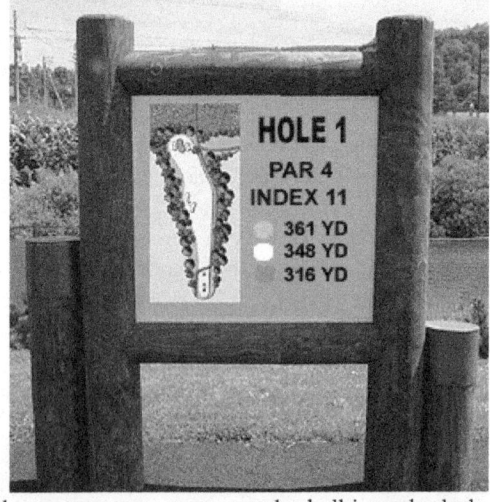

The second row, 'PAR 4', tells you that a skilled golfer should require 4 strokes to successfully sink his ball into this hole. The par of a hole is defined by the distance from tee to green. Typical values from the Ladies Tee are:
Par 3 - 210 yards and below
Par 4 - 211 to 400 yards
Par 5 - 401 to 575 yards
Par 6 (rare) - 575 yards or more

Par is also the theoretical number of strokes that an expert golfer should require for playing the ball into any given hole. The expert golfer is expected to reach the green in two strokes under par (in regulation) and then use two putts to get the ball into the hole. Many 18-hole courses have approximately four par-three, ten par-four, and four par-five holes. The total par of an 18-hole course is usually around 72.

The third row, 'INDEX 11', shows you the relatively difficulty of the hole. Index 1 is the most difficult hole and Index 18 is the easiest. This hole is ranked 11th which is quite an easy hole.

Following the Index are three colored circles with corresponding numbers. The numbers indicate the distance from each of the colored tee boxes. Some courses have four tee boxes and may show distances in meters.

Tee Box

The tee box is where you start off at each hole. It's not actually a box, but a virtual rectangle formed by two colored markers. The color corresponds to that on the layout board, generally 'blue' for low handicappers, 'white' or 'yellow' for average and high handicappers and 'red' for ladies.

Golfer having just teed off from Tee Box onto Fairway

If you draw a straight line connecting both markers, you have the front line of the tee box. The back line is at a distance of two club-lengths. You can place your ball anywhere between these two lines and in between the two markers. This is the only place where you are allowed to "tee up" your ball before taking a swing at it.

According to golf rules, only the ball can be placed inside the tee box. You may stand outside of the tee box to hit the ball.

Our red tee box is sometimes considerably in front of the mens' white tee box, this is to level the playing field in case men and women play in the same group as the difference in distance compensates for the guys longer drives. Guys usually complain about this as unfair.

Fairway

When hitting your ball, you want it to stop on the fairway. This is an area of closely mowed grass along the way from the tee box to the green. A fairway is like a passageway to the green, clearly distinguishable from the rough and from hazards (see below). It isn't always continuous and it varies in width and direction. A bend of the fairway to the right or left is called a 'dog leg'.

Fairway is guarded by Rough on left and right

Rough

As we all know, where you want to hit the ball may not be where it actually lands. At some point in the game, you may find your ball flying into the long grass or trees. The collective name for these undesirable areas is 'the rough'. You will see rough on either side of the fairway. It's harder to hit the ball out of a rough than from the fairway. If the rough is really bad, hit the ball on to the nearest fairway.

Most rough will include trees. These areas are also called jungles. Surprisingly, some jungles are preferable to the rough before them. That's because the trees discourage long grass from growing underneath. You will often see bare patches of ground that offer a better shot than the thick grass beyond.

Hazards

Hazards are traps purposely designed to increase the difficulty of the course. The number of hazards corresponds to the difficulty and challenge of a particular course. There are two kinds of hazards.

Water Hazard

As the name implies, a water hazard is one that contains water. They can be man-made or natural ponds filled with water. Natural hazards include rivers, lakes, creeks or the sea.

Normal Water Hazard

A Normal water hazard lies across the fairway and is defined by yellow stakes.

Lateral Water Hazard

Golf courses can also contain a lateral water hazard. This stretch of water lies alongside the fairway and is marked by red stakes.

Bunkers

Bunkers or sand traps are pits filled with sand. You'll find fairway bunkers placed in strategic positions along the fairway to trap your ball. If you're unfortunate enough to hit your ball into one, you can

walk in and hit your ball out without paying a penalty. However, you're not allowed to touch the sand with your club before your actual stroke.

Bunkers that guard the green are called greenside bunkers and courses usually contain more than one.

Pot bunker - note the very high and steep front lip

Surprisingly, some golfers prefer to play from the bunker than from the rough surrounding the green. Experienced golfers can control bunker shots.

Green

No golf course is complete without the green. This refers to the lovely piece of ground where you hope to find your ball after a swing.

The grass in a green differs from that in the fairway or rough. It can be either Bermuda grass or Bent grass. The type of grass will influence the speed of the ball. The grass of the putting green is cut very short so that a ball can roll over distances of several meters. "To putt" means to play a stroke on the green where the

ball does not leave the ground. The direction of growth of individual blades of grass affects the rolling of a golf ball and is called the grain. The hole must have a diameter of 108 mm and a depth of at least 100 mm. Its position on the green is not static and may be changed from day to day. This hole on the green has a flag on a pole positioned in it so that it may be seen from some distance (but not necessarily from the tee). It is also termed "the pin".

No two greens are alike. Some greens are quite flat and easy to putt, whereas others have slopes to test your skills. In this territory, you are playing a different game entirely. No more of those hefty swings and chops. This area requires finesse and will test your nerves. This is the game within a game that will determine the final outcome.

The Flagstick

It is often difficult to see the hole because of the long distance. This is where the flagstick comes into play. Basically, it's a long pole with a flag or plastic placard on top. The color of the flag indicates where the hole is relative to the green. Red is used for holes located in the front part of the green. White is used for holes located in the middle and blue is used for holes at the back end of the green. The difference between red and blue holes may require the use of another club. Some clubs may use a different set of colors.

Hole

There is nothing sweeter than hearing the sound of your ball dropping into the hole. The hole, or cup, has a diameter of four and a quarter inches. It must be at least four inches deep.

You have to sink the ball into the hole in order to complete your play. Otherwise, you will be penalized.

Borders of the Golf Course

The borders of a course are marked as such, and beyond them is "out of bounds", that is, ground from which a ball must not be played. Special rules apply to certain man-made objects on the course (obstructions) and to ground in abnormal condition.

The Driving Range

At most golf courses there are additional facilities that are not part of the course itself. Often there is a practice range, usually with practice greens, bunkers, and a driving area (where long shots can be practiced). There may even be a practice course (which is often easier to play or shorter than other golf courses). A golf school is often associated to a course or club.

No matter if you're a beginner or a seasoned golfer, you should practice at a driving range instead of a golf course. Even if you have already taken lessons, you need to reinforce what you have learned. The driving range is the best place to accomplish this.

In case this is your first time out on the range, here are a few pointers to observe:

1. **Don't Use Your Own Balls.** Never practice with your own golf balls unless you want to donate them to the range. You can't retrieve a hit ball.

2. **Buy Practice Balls.** Purchase practice balls from the range attendant or ball dispensing machine. If you buy them from a machine, hang a bucket on the hook below the ball drop. Once you insert the tokens, the machine will dispense the relevant number of balls.

3. **Choose A Bay.** A driving range has several bays or stalls numbering from 12 to a few dozen. These bays are separated by partitions. Try to choose a bay located far from other golfers so you don't distract them.

4. **Tee Up.** Some driving ranges have automatic ball machines that tee-up your ball if you step on a pedal. Otherwise, you have to manually tee-up.

5. **Synthetic Mats.** Most driving ranges use synthetic mats or artificial grass that has rubber tees for your balls. If there is no tee, insert one into the available holes. Just lift up the mat and insert the tee through the bottom.

6. **Natural Grass.** If you practice on natural grass, you need more room because of the divots you'll create. Don't hit from the exact same spot.

7. **Use All Your Clubs.** Since you are new to the range, practice using all your clubs to get used to the feel of each one. In the latter part of your session, concentrate on one or two clubs to practice your swing.

8. **Don't Show Off.** As you search for an open bay, you may notice a golfer driving his ball really far. Many golfers do this just to impress others. Resist the temptation and concentrate on practicing.

9. **Different From Actual Course.** Be aware that a driving range is never the same as a real golf course. Even with natural grass, they can't simulate a real situation. You always perform better on a range than a golf course because you're more relaxed and you're repeating the same swing. Unfortunately, you don't have this luxury on an actual course.

Now to the practice part:

The driving range is the place to practice your game, shot by shot. Regular practice at the golf driving range will benefit every golfer's game. Having said that, many people don't get the full benefit out of a trip to the range. Many times golfers on the range just hit one ball after the other, often without looking where the shot went. In my eyes this is a waste of effort.

You should hit your practice shot, look at it, analyze it and make adjustments as needed. This way fewer balls can actually lead to faster progression of your game, and it's also a lot less stressful.

To get you started here are five practice tips for the next time you hit the range:

1. Do not just knock balls into the air for the mere benefit of seeing them fly. Instead, have a goal of exactly what you want out of each session. Decide what you want to achieve and focus on that.

2. Always aim for a target, whether it be someplace on the artificial green, a yardage marker sign, or a patch of grass.

3. Learn when to stop. When you come to the point on the driving range when you have reached your goal for the day, learn when to stop. Hitting too many balls can lead to injury and boredom.

4. Give equal practice time to your short game as you do your long-distance shots.

5. When practicing your short shots, never hit them from the same spot each and every time. Vary your length and distances for faster progression. Also vary the directions so that you are not always aligned the same way.

General Golf Course Architecture and Design

While no two courses are alike, many can be classified into one of the following broad categories:

Links courses: the most traditional type of golf course, of which some century-old examples have survived in the British Isles, located in coastal areas, on sandy soil, often amid dunes, with few water hazards and few if any trees.

Parkland courses: typical inland courses, often resembling traditional British parks, with lawn-like fairways and many trees.

Heath land – a more open, less manicured inland course often featuring gorse and heather and typically less wooded than "parkland" courses. Examples include Woodhall Spa in England or Gleneagles in Scotland.

Desert courses: a rather recent invention, popular in parts of the USA and in the Middle East. Desert courses require heavy irrigation for maintenance of the turf, leading to concerns about the ecological consequences of excessive water consumption. A desert course also violates the widely accepted principle of golf course architecture that an aesthetically pleasing course should require minimal alteration of the existing landscape. Nevertheless, many players enjoy the unique experience of playing golf in the desert.

Environmental Impact

A major result of modern equipment is that today's players can hit the ball much further than previously. In a concern for safety, modern golf course architects have had to lengthen and widen their design envelope. This has led to a 10% increase in the amount of area that is required for golf courses today. At the same time, water restrictions placed by many communities have forced the modern architect to limit the amount of maintained turf grass on the golf course. While most modern 18-hole golf courses occupy as much as 60 ha (150 acres) of land, the average course has 30 ha (75 acres) of maintained turf.

Environmental concerns over the use of land for golf courses have grown over the past 30 years. People are concerned about the amount of water and types of chemicals used as well as the destruction of wetlands and other environmentally important areas.

These, along with health and cost concerns, have led to significant research into more environmentally sound practices and turf grasses. The modern golf course superintendent is well trained in the uses of these practices and grasses. This has led to reductions in amount of chemicals and water used on courses. The turf on golf courses is an excellent filter for water and has been used in many communities to cleanse grey water.

While many people continue to oppose golf courses for environmental reasons, there are others who feel that they are beneficial for the community and the environment as they provide corridors for migrating animals and sanctuaries for birds and other wildlife.

Golf courses are built on many different types of land, including sandy areas along coasts, abandoned farms, strip mines and quarries, deserts and forests. Many Western countries have instituted significant environmental restrictions on where and how courses can be built.

In some parts of the world, attempts to build courses and resorts have led to significant protests along with vandalism and violence by both sides. Although golf is a relatively minor issue compared to other land ethics questions, it has symbolic importance as it is a game normally associated with the wealthier Westernized population, and the culture of colonization and globalization of non-native land ethics. Resisting golf tourism and golf's expansion has become an objective of some land reform movements, especially in the Philippines and Indonesia.

In Saudi Arabia, American experts have played golf on courses of nothing more than oil-covered sand. However, in some cities such as Dhahran, modern grass golf courses have been built.

Equipment Overview for Lady Golfers

Enjoying the game of golf requires many kinds of skills. Sometimes a shot requires distance and sometimes accuracy. Some shots we hit from a tee, some we play from short grass and sometimes even from oh-so-dreaded places like rough, sand and dry dirt (hardpan). Each of such situations will benefits from a different club you use. Based on our abilities, some shots will be relatively easy and some will be frustratingly difficult.

Case in point: If the challenge is a 120 yard carry over water to a rather tight pin on a small green, the proper choice of club for a beginner, intermediate or advanced Lady Golfer will be different. The beginner will need all the help and forgiveness possible ("...*I swear, if I make this shot I'll be a good person for the rest of my life...*"). The intermediate may need a little less forgiveness but still wants to be comfortable with their club. The advanced player may want more subtle characteristics of feel and clubhead response that a beginner can't even imagine (... and still pledge to become a better person if the shot works out). In the past all three were left with only a few club choices, but - thankfully - today there are many more.

Types of Golf Clubs

There are four major categories of clubs: woods, hybrids, irons, and putters. Wedges resemble irons and may also be counted among these. A golfer is allowed to carry up to fourteen clubs during a round - the limit defined by the official rules of the Royal and Ancient Golf Club of St Andrews (R&A) and the United States Golf Association (USGA).

While it is possible to play a range of different shots using only one club, modifying only the speed and direction of swing, this is not a particularly successful technique. It is far easier to keep the swing as constant as possible and achieve different lengths and characteristics of ball flight using a different club for each shot.

To facilitate the choice of a club for any particular situation, all irons (and many woods and wedges) come in sets of similar clubs graded by loft (see below), shaft length, and weight. Clubs are numbered for identification with the smallest numbers indicating the lowest loft.

Various clubs are designed with the face having differing loft (the angle between a vertical plane and the clubface when the club is at rest). Perhaps with the exception of tee shots, it is loft that makes a golf ball leave the ground, not an upward direction of swing: for some shots with a particularly high trajectory such as pitches, the club actually hits the ball in a motion, and with most other shots the motion is more or less horizontal. Typically, the greater the loft, the higher and shorter the resulting ball trajectory.

A typical set of clubs may consist of irons 3 to 9, three wedges, woods 1, 3, and 5, and a putter.

Which Clubs are most important?

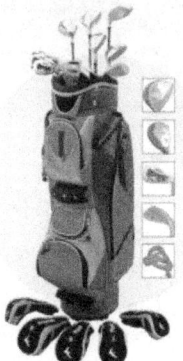

As mentioned, golf requires several kinds of shots - drives, long approach shots, short approach shots, pitches, chips, sand shots, putts and a variety of so called trouble shots.

By far the most frequent shot is a putt. For an average golfer (both male and female), the putter is used more than twice as much as any other club. Statistically, if a golfer shoots a score of 100, 35% - 40% of those strokes will be putts. So, quite obviously, the putter is the most important club you carry.

Generally, for most lady golfers the driver (also called the #1 wood) is used the next most often club, roughly on 14 out of 18 tee shots in average depending on ability level and course requirements. A good drive makes the rest of the shots on that hole easier. A lousy drive means, well, you know what… That makes the driver a very important club.

For players who have a hard time hitting the green in a regulation number of strokes, the wedges may be the second most used category of clubs. Even on a good day a beginner may spend a 15 to 20 strokes chipping up to the green.

The remaining challenges in a round will utilize the rest of the clubs in your set. It is likely that no one club will be used more than a few times. This means, in terms of club usage, the putter, driver and wedges are clearly used the most frequently while the rest of the clubs will bring up the rear.

Now let's look at the different clubs in more detail:

The Driver / 1 Wood

Take a look into the bag of any golfer. Chances are you'll see something in there with the word titanium on it. In recent years, the Periodic Table of Elements' 22nd element, Ti, has catapulted into the forefront as golf's most precious metal. It's used in the manufacturing of putters, irons, and shafts - even balls! However, nowhere is it more prevalent than in an oversized driver. Reason: it's very strong and very light. As a result, manufacturers are able to make oversize clubheads out of titanium and still maintain the same weight as a traditional size clubhead.

Modern Ladies Titanium Driver

Titanium heads are usually 1/3 larger than most wooden or metal drivers or woods. Also, because titanium is lighter, manufacturers can make the shafts longer as well. In fact many titanium drivers are 2-3 inches longer than most other metal drivers. The result is simple. A bigger clubhead doesn't twist as much on off-center hits and a longer shaft translates into a bigger swing arc - both of these are key ingredients to added length off the tee. The maximum size currenlt allowed is 460 cc, and there are also limitations to the physical dimensions of the club head.

Today's Driver is Much Better

Years ago, golfers played with persimmon and laminated woods. In truth, when these clubs were struck properly, nothing felt better. However, there are only so many Annika Sorenstams out there and these clubs were anything but forgiving on mis-hits. When you hit today's oversized titanium driver off the heel or toe, you still come away with a salvageable shot. Since most golfers miss more often than they hit the ball perfectly, the larger titanium heads have big advantages. They make the ball go a greater distance on off-center hits. So with titanium, it's not that the material itself that makes the ball go farther, it's that the bigger head makes your misses go farther. When your grandfather mis-hit his persimmon club, he could lose 50 yards of distance. In that sense, titanium and oversized-head technology has made the average player better. It has also allowed senior players to keep up with the youngsters off the tee. Titanium and other metal drivers are also more durable than wooden woods.

The High Cost of Titanium

Titanium is the fourth most available element in the world. It's found in beach sand throughout the world, especially in Australia and China. Despite this abundance, Ti drivers are more expensive than steel models. That's because it's very difficult to manufacture a titanium head. Mining titanium from beach sand is not an easy process. As a result, the raw material cost is higher than steel.

Secondly, titanium must be cast in a vacuum, a chamber without air. Even if done properly, this is expensive, because many clubheads don't come out perfect and must be destroyed. The shaft is also a factor. Most titanium woods are made using very lightweight graphite shafts. The lighter the shaft, the harder they are to make and the more expensive they become. Of course, some of titanium's high price is the result of marketing and advertising costs.

Titanium Might Suit You

Initially, these drivers were developed to help the average player or short hitter get added distance off the tee. For this type of player, titanium is ideal. However, even professionals have benefited from titanium. Today's tour players who would have had below-average length 15 years ago are now keeping up with their playing partners.

Pick the Right Loft for You

When you're spending hard-earned money on a product, make sure that it perfectly fits your game. Don't automatically purchase a driver just because it's a well known brand and it's on sale. Make sure you understand your game. Remember, the greater the loft, the easier it will be to control. A higher lofted club (i.e. 12 degrees loft) gives you more carry but less roll, and vice versa. It's important to note that a titanium driver hits the ball higher than you might expect. This is due to the center of gravity being farther back in the clubhead and the shaft being longer. Many times a 9-degree titanium driver will produce the same ball flight as a 10.5-degree stainless metal wood. Because titanium clubs are longer, it's important to choose a club that gives you the best combination of accuracy and distance. Distance is useless without accuracy. Remember, the longer the shaft, the more difficult any club is to control. As a beginner you should select a driver with a deeper face to promote added role and a more controllable, boring trajectory--all important to added length off the tee. However, if you already hit a low ball, take this into account. For example, select a deep-face driver with a higher loft.

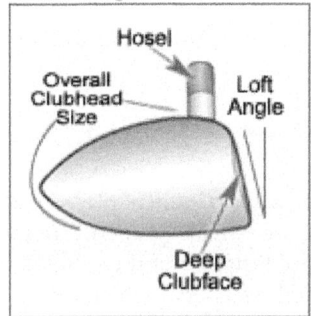
Anatomy of a Driver

Choose the Right Shaft

The most important component of any golf club is the shaft. In a nutshell, steel gives you more accuracy than graphite. Graphite shafts give you more distance. That's because steel flexes less than graphite at impact. The only time this isn't true is when manufacturers add material into the graphite (boron, etc.) to make it flex less or perform more like steel. Graphite is ideal for woman and senior players for many reasons. It's lighter, absorbs the shock of impact better, and generally has a lower flex point to help you get the ball airborne. Because it's lighter, it's also better for those players experiencing back problems. A titanium head combined with a steel shaft is for the golfer who has plenty of strength but wants more forgiveness on mis-hits.

Square Club Heads benefit Lady Golfers

A more recent development came with the introduction of the 'square' clubhead. The first companies to introduce them to the markets were Nike and Callaway Golf.

The main benefit of the square shape is the substantial increase of its moment of inertia (MOI). In layman terms, MOI refers to the resistance to twisting of the clubhead when struck. Let's say that you hit the ball with the toe of your driver. A low MOI clubhead will twist on impact and send the ball way off to the right (for RH players). In contrast, a high MOI clubhead will twist a much less and you should be getting a lot closer to your intended target line. In other words, the higher the MOI is the more forgiving the club will be on miss hits. The square shape design increases both horizontal and vertical stability which in turn results in a very high MOI, thus assuring a long and accurate shot.

Square Driver and Fairway Wood

NOTE: New Ladies Driver models enter the market all the time, so please make sure you visit **http://bit.ly/LadyGolfersGuide** on a regular basis. There we will introduce you to the newest clubs and trends.

Fairway Woods

The second shot on a par-5 has been called the most boring shot in golf. Yet, the club that most players use for that shot, makes most players face two challenges with this shot: to hit it farther and to hit it straighter. Outside of working to make your golf swing more effective, which you should be doing, the fairway wood can help to solve the farther/straighter problem. It can probably also save you a couple of strokes.

The New Era

There was a time when woods were made out of...wood. In fact, these were the clubs of choice during the feathery-ball era, which – as described earlier - lasted from the 15th Century to the middle of the 19th Century. With the introduction of the Taylor Made Pittsburgh Persimmon metal-headed driver in 1979, golf club design changed again. Although this club wasn't immediately embraced by purists because of its sound at impact and nontraditional appearance, it nonetheless allowed club designers greater latitude.

Lady's Fairway Woods

With metal (usually steel), the designer can easily make the clubhead larger or smaller, add runners to the sole, or build out the toe--all in an effort to make the club perform better. This helps you to hit the ball straighter and with more confidence. Steel also has a higher strength-to-weight ratio than wood, allowing the club maker to use less material without sacrificing strength. The result is a lighter, easier-to-swing clubhead. Even more, to help the club perform better and be more forgiving, weight is moved to the perimeter of the clubhead to help it square at impact and be more stable on off-center hits.

Your Best Friend

The Fairway Wood can make your wandering tee shot a little less problematic and the long par-4s a little more reachable. And other than the short irons, the fairway woods are the easiest clubs to hit. Most mid-to-high-handicap players have much more confidence in a fairway wood than either their driver or a long iron.

The ease in hitting is accomplished by two design features. The larger clubhead, when compared to an iron, provides greater stability because it is less likely to twist through impact. This helps you return the clubface to square at impact and produces straighter ball flight.

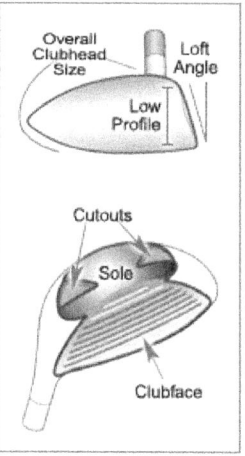
Anatomy of a Fairway Wood

The loft of a fairway wood is typically 15 degrees for a standard 3-wood, 19 degrees for a 5-wood, and 24 degrees for a 7-wood. The loft of the 5-wood corresponds to a 2-iron, and the 7-wood to a 4-iron. Many intermediate golfers are using these woods as reliable substitutes for the corresponding irons.

Here are some of the technical advances you can expect to find in this new generation of metalwoods:

• **Low center of gravity**

Because a metalwood is hollow, the weight is concentrated to the sole and the outside of the clubhead to help get the ball airborne and increase the sweetspot.

• **Stronger lofts**

The low center of gravity means the manufacturer can use stronger lofts without compromising trajectory. This translates to added distance.

• **Miracle metals**

In the last few years, new-age steels and titanium have been used to provide even more advantages. These light, strong materials allow the club designer to maintain the strength and integrity of the clubhead and place yet more weight on the sole, the back, the heel, and the toe for greater stability through impact.

• **Inserts**

A change of rules in '92 allowed for inserts in metal clubs (irons and woods). For instance, some clubs now have forged steel inserts in the face. This harder-hitting surface provides greater impact force and a better "feel" for the player. A complaint among better players was that metalwoods didn't provide response on off-center hits. The insert helps to combine the advantages of a perimeter-weighted metalwood with the more traditional response at impact.

• **Trouble clubs**

Many fairway woods are designed as trouble clubs. Instead of a flat sole, these clubs have a rounded or convex sole, and some employ cutouts or bulges to ensure better contact in the rough or from fairway bunkers. This can prove as invaluable to scoring well as any club in the bag.

NOTE: New Ladies Fairway Woods enter the market all the time, so please make sure you visit http://bit.ly/LadyGolfersGuide on a regular basis. There we will introduce you to the newest clubs and trends.

Irons

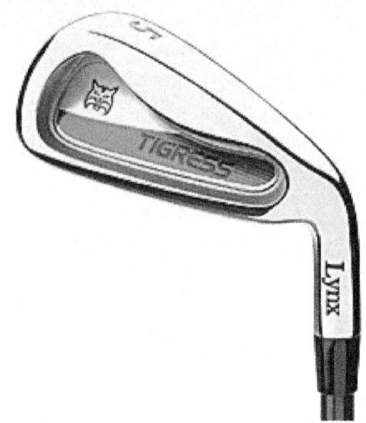

Lynx Tigress Iron Set

Having a good Set of Irons that you can trust is very comforting. Sure, driving the ball is fun, but in a round of golf it's the irons you count on to get you on the green and in position to do well. The good news is that modern technology has made irons easier to hit than ever. This section will help you learn the basics of iron design, how they've improved, and which clubs are best suited for your game.

Most iron sets consist of a 3-iron through pitching wedge (listed as 3-PW). This accounts for 8 of the 14 clubs you can carry according to the Rules of Golf, leaving room for a putter and three woods. Some players substitute a high-lofted wood for the 3-iron because they find it easier to hit. This is a good strategy. However, stronger players who don't have a problem getting the ball up may still prefer to use the more accurate long irons.

Here's a guide to the key features of today's irons:

• **Blade versus cavity-back**

A blade iron offers a smaller hitting surface and a thin top-line (portion of the clubhead viewed at address). It also has more mass behind the middle of the clubhead, sometimes called a "muscle-back," that gives a very soft feeling when hit properly. In contrast, a cavity-back or perimeter-weighted club has more weight around the outside edges of the clubhead to produce a larger sweetspot. The easiest-hitting irons of all generally have a large cavity-back, thick top-line, and oversize clubface. But increasingly, clubmakers are offering designs that incorporate the forgiving benefits of cavity-back in a blade style with a thinner top-line. For many traditionalist golfers, this is the answer.

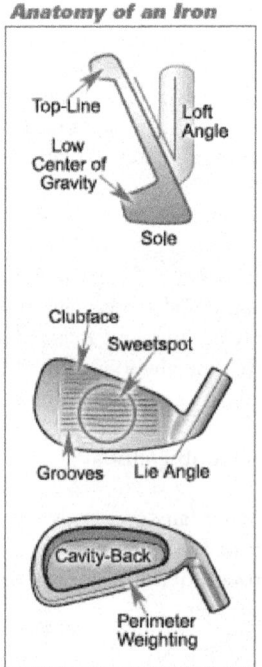

- **Casting versus forging**

Up until the early 1970s, forged steel clubheads accounted for more than 90% of all irons made. This model involves hammering and shaping the clubhead. Now, investment casting has taken over as the primary manufacturing method. Casting, in which the metal is poured into a mold, costs less and makes it easier to produce the complex shapes of today's perimeter-weighted, cavity-back designs within tight specifications. However, forging is not likely to disappear because many golfers believe it offers better feel and ball "workability." It also offers a cleaner look for the tradition-minded golfer.

- **Hosel offset**

This is measured from the leading edge of the hosel (where the shaft enters the clubhead) to the farthest front portion of the clubface. Why is it important? A club with offset contacts the ball later than a club without offset. This helps "square" the clubface at impact and reduces the tendency to slice (ball going right for right-handed golfers).

- **Progressive weighting**

This involves placing a heavier material, such as copper or tungsten, in the sole of lower-lofted irons. This helps lower the center of gravity and get the ball in the air. Progressive weighting is generally eliminated in the shorter irons to help produce a lower, flatter trajectory.

Other Iron Features

- *Grooves or scoring lines*

Grooves add spin and control to the ball's flight. An iron with no grooves causes the ball to "squirt" off the face. Backspin may decrease distance slightly but greatly enhances control. Karsten Solheim, legendary founder of Ping, brought attention to the value of grooves when players of his clubs with larger, sharper grooves began showing superior control--especially out of rough lies. The USGA strictly controls the depth and distance between scoring lines on the clubface to ensure fairness.

- *Lie*

This is the angle of the sole (bottom) of the club as it relates to the shaft. Too "flat" a lie places the heel of the club in the air, while too upright a lie angle causes the toe to be in the air at address. Lie angle for all custom clubs should be tailored to your body.

• *Loft*

This is the clubface angle relative to the shaft, and determines the trajectory of your shots. It varies from about 22 degrees in a 3-iron for a lower, longer trajectory to 64 degrees in a wedge for short, high shots.

• *Satin finish vs. polish or chrome*

This is merely a cosmetic question. A satin finish can be very attractive, but in general has a duller appearance than polished or chrome-finish clubheads.

• *Sole*

This is the very bottom part of the clubhead. If you look closely at the sole of your club, you'll notice it has a slight curvature from toe to heel and from leading edge to trailing edge. This "camber" or "radius sole" makes it easier to hit consistent shots. Sole width is another factor. A narrower sole works better from fairway and tight lie conditions while a wider sole is better for plush lies.

> NOTE: New Irons enter the market all the time, so please make sure you visit http://bit.ly/LadyGolfersGuide on a regular basis. There we will introduce you to the newest clubs and trends.

Wedges

Wedges have come a long way in recent years. New lofts and clubhead shapes have prompted many players to carry as many as four wedges, for every conceivable situation around the green. If you're just carrying the old reliable pitching wedge, you're missing out on some simple ways to lower your scores. After all, more than 70% of your game is played from 100 yards or closer.

Cleveland Lady CG-11 W-series Wedge

How Wedges Work

All wedges are characterized by high lofts (typically 45-60 degrees) to increase trajectory, and significant sole weighting to help you penetrate sand or grass. Most are also heavier overall. But that's where the similarities end. Each wedge type has its own characteristics, making it suited to a particular distance or lie.

Anatomy of a Wedge

One important characteristic is the bounce angle. As the name implies, this feature enables the clubhead to "bounce" out of the sand or rough without digging in. If you look at the sole of a sand wedge, for instance, you'll notice that the trailing edge hangs below the leading edge. Bounce is the angle formed by the leading edge and the ground. This tiny angle (maximum 16 degrees) doesn't sound like much, but it's what makes it worthwhile for you to carry a good sand wedge in your bag. Without bounce, you may just stay in that bunker forever. And in general, less experienced players should use a club with more bounce in soft or fluffy lies.

As with putters, wedges are the focus of a lot of experimentation in materials and **face inserts**. Clubheads are often made of softer materials, such as copper or beryllium alloy, to increase feel and touch around the green. Some are intended to rust over time, giving a unique appearance. Manufacturers have also devised unique ways to impart precise spin on the ball and help it hold the green upon landing. The most basic treatment is scoring or sandblasting of the face. U-shaped grooves, which are square at the bottom, are also used. Still another method is to use a different material altogether in the face, such as a super-hard diamond compound.

One major development has been the introduction of the "gap" or "dual" wedge. As manufacturers decreased the loft of the typical pitching wedge to increase its distance (a little

35

sleight of hand), they created a "gap" between it and the next longest club, the sand wedge (see graphic below). Thus, in order of distance, the progression is as follows: pitching wedge, gap wedge, sand wedge, and lob wedge. They are described here in order.

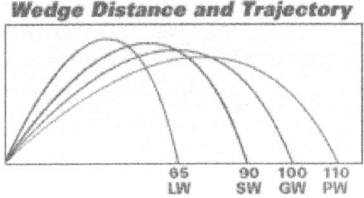

Pitching Wedge

This club has typically 45-49 degrees of loft and is used for longer approach shots (about 110 yards for men, 90 yards for women). Because it's most often hit from the grass, it has minimal bounce (2-5 degrees). In fact, a lot of bounce would be undesirable in this club, because it would make it more difficult to get the leading edge under the ball, causing you to skull it.

Gap Wedge

This club has typically 49-54 degrees of loft and is used for shots of about 100 yards for men, or about 95 yards for women. Bounce is typically 5-12 degrees. But don't pick a gap wedge at random. Choose a loft that divides the "gap" evenly between your pitching and sand wedges. For instance, if you have a 48-degree PW and a 56-degree SW, buy a gap wedge with 52 degrees. This club is also known as a "dual" or "attack" wedge.

Sand Wedge

This club has typically 54-57 degrees of loft and is used for shots of about 90 yards maximum for men, or about 80 yards for women. It also has the most unique clubhead of the bunch, with lots of bounce (10-16 degrees) and another feature called heel-toe camber. This is what gives the sand wedge an oval shape on the bottom of the face. Finally, sand wedges have more sole width (the distance between the leading and trailing edge). All these features are designed to reduce the risk of digging in.

Lob Wedge

This club has 57 or more degrees of loft and is used for shots of about 65 yards maximum for men, or 60 yards for women. These clubs, also called "finesse" wedges, are for "touch" shots around the green that need to get into the air quickly and land softly. Bounce is minimal (0-10 degrees), because in these situations there is generally very little room under the ball, and a tiny error can make the club bounce off the ground and cause a skulled shot. It has less sole width and a sharp leading edge. One reason many players like this club is because it allows a full, unimpeded swing to cover a short distance, rather than making you rely on an abbreviated swing. The ball flies short and high.

NOTE: New Ladies Wedges enter the market all the time, so please make sure you visit **http://bit.ly/LadyGolfersGuide** on a regular basis. There we will introduce you to the newest clubs and trends.

Hybrid Clubs

Snake Eyes Viper-W Hybrid

If you follow golf on television or subscribe to golf magazines then you have likely witnessed the mounting discussion surrounding Hybrid (sometimes referred to as utility) clubs. The buzz is starting to spread, and you are starting to hear more about hybrids because they are becoming the hottest and most popular club to carry in your bag. Unlike some clubs that are specifically designed for certain players or skill levels, hybrids are suited for both, recreational players and touring pros.

The word hybrid means something that is of mixed origin or composition. In golf, they have taken ideologies of both a wood and iron design and combined them, to manufacture some of the most forgiving and easiest clubs to hit to date. Features you will find on the hybrid are:

- Flatness of the face on the hybrid wood. Woods have a curve on the face but the hybrids are flat just like an iron.

- Weighting that is distributed throughout the club like an iron or fairway wood. Most woods have the focus of the weight distributed towards the front.

- A wide sole like a fairway wood, with a club length similar to an iron rather than a wood.

The main idea behind the hybrid wood is to be interchangeable and utilize the characteristics of both an iron and a wood. The resultant club is typically easier to hit with less effort than a traditional long and lower lofted iron. The term "long iron" normally describes all the clubs from a two iron through five.

There are multiple reasons why many recreational golfers struggle with long iron shots and the goal of the hybrid wood is to make it easier for you. The most common problems are:

- Not being able to make a complete shoulder turn on the backswing.

- Swinging too hard and throwing off tempo.

- Lower lofted clubs are harder to hit.

The elite players who do all the right things with long irons save strokes during the average round, but the majority of players struggle with them, and now have an alternative in the hybrid club. The long narrow face and a wide sole of hybrid clubs utilizes a low center of gravity cog, which helps players with slower swing speeds launch the ball with little effort, making a hybrid club similar to playing a wood in that it lends itself to the sweeping style swing rather than picking the ball off the turf with greater effort as a traditional iron. Effectively, all players benefit, but particularly grateful are those players who have lost swing speed due to age, injury or other physically conditions that have prevented them from making a full shoulder turn on the backswing. Hybrids allow for a shorter back swing while launching the same distance you are use to experiencing with a wood.

The face of a hybrid is manufactured out of harder 17-4 stainless steel, similar to a fairway wood, which helps with the ball compression and forgiveness of the club. The hardness of the metal allows a slower swing speed to produce distance that you would normally see with a faster swing speed. Not only will you see longer distances from the hybrid wood, you should see more accuracy because the hybrid allows for a greater margin for error. All this from a club that is shorter and lighter than its performance-matching counterparts.

Many players using Hybrids are not only replacing long irons but are using them as fairway woods as well. Some of the loft angles on Hybrid clubs match those of a 3 and 5 wood but are shorter, lighter and more versatile.

Hybrids are extremely versatile and can be used easily from the fairway, rough or tee, and they are a great stroke saver. If you suffer, as many do, from the long iron blues, you should consider a hybrid to compliment your game.

NOTE: New Ladies Hybrid Clubs enter the market all the time, so please make sure you visit http://bit.ly/LadyGolfersGuide on a regular basis. There we will introduce you to the newest clubs and trends.

Putters

The Putter is one piece of equipment with which you can truly express yourself. Beside a colorful shirt or a jaunty cap, the putter best matches the person because the putter must match the player's putting style.

Mostly, this is due to "feel": an elusive quality that's nearly impossible to describe, yet most golfers understand it. Feel doesn't just mean how the putter physically feels to the touch or when stroking a putt. It's the response you gets when holding the putter, taking a practice stroke, drawing the putter back, and making contact with the ball. Feel takes the putting stroke and transforms the act from science to art. For sure, much of this takes place between the ears. But the right Putter can certainly help. Head materials, head designs, and grips are just a few of the tools club makers use to achieve the right feel.

Ladies Mallet-style Putters

Head Shape

The greatest variations in putter design are in the head itself. From blade, to mallet, to oversize, the putter head has included all things great and small. The blade appears thin when you look down from the top, and it has no material behind it. A traditional blade putter head is about the thickness of your finger. This type of putter is less forgiving on off-center hits, but provides accuracy. Many blades now retain a thin top line appearance, but have material on the back of the putter head that's been hollowed out in a cavity-back design to reduce twisting at contact.

A mallet is larger and wider than a blade, often having a broad surface that contacts the ground.

Ladies Blade-style Putter

Some models include alignment lines to assist in lining up a putt. They can be as simple as a notch in the center of the top line of the putter, or as elaborate as a system of lines and arrows pointing in the direction that you'll be hitting the ball. Some people find them distracting, but these lines used in conjunction with the trademark on the ball can aid putts tremendously.

Head Materials

Most putter heads are made of stainless or carbon steel. Bronze and brass are also used, and provide a softer feel. Aluminum is also used for a soft feel and lightweight. Graphite, polymers and other plastics are used to make a putter head that is very resilient and very light. These materials generally make the head more expensive.

Inserts

Putter heads have been the focus of a lot of experimentation in materials. Some have lightweight composite inserts in the face, which, by ratio, places more weight in the toe and heel. Inserts are a relatively new design element in putters. They're intended to provide greater response at contact. Most inserts are a synthetic material; although, some are a softer metal such as aluminum. Some companies have experimented with rubber faces, aluminum honeycomb-like structures, and the like. The insert conforms to the ball on contact and generates a softer feel through the shaft and to your hands. The result is a more controlled roll. Sometimes, the face of metal putter heads are milled--material is cut away to achieve an extremely flat surface and maximized feel.

Weight

Weight is the greatest contributor to how the putter feels in your hands. You notice it the moment you pick it up. A putter head that is too light contributes to a "handsy" putting style where the hands control the stroke, making the putter head pass through the contact zone too quickly. This usually causes putts to run long. A heavy putter head creates drag in the stroke. The putter head passes through the contact zone too slowly, causing putts to come up short.

In general, a mallet putter is somewhat heavier. Steel putter heads are lighter than bronze, brass, or aluminum models. Overall, it's better to err on the side of a lighter putter. A heavier putter is less consistent for you over the course of 18 holes.

Balance

When a putter head is balanced, it resists twisting at impact, which helps impart a more consistent roll to the ball. To test this, balance a putter on your finger by placing your finger under the shaft near the putter head. With a face-balanced putter, the clubface remains nearly parallel to the ground. A face-balanced putter can be achieved through a cavity-back design, where more weight is placed in the heel and toe.

Length

Length should be determined by your putting stance. The more you crouch over the ball, the shorter the putter needs to be. The more you stand up, the longer the putter should be. Most putters are 34 or 35 inches long. Try one of each. Keep in mind that a longer putter is more difficult to control and may not impart as much feel.

Loft

As much as it appears that the face of a putter is straight up and down, there is a slight degree of loft on every putter--usually about four degrees. Loft helps the ball to roll properly. On the putting stroke, the ball is actually lifted slightly at impact, skids a bit due to backspin, and then begins to roll over and toward the target.

Shafts
Putters can either be center shafted (the shaft connects near the middle of the putter head) or heel shafted (the shaft connects near the heel). An offset shaft helps set up a proper stroke. In this design, a bend in the hosel (where the shaft enters the clubhead) or shaft helps keep your hands ahead of the ball, promoting a smoother stroke. Shafts can also be in hosel (the hosel surrounds the shaft) or over hosel (the shaft surround the hosel). With some models, there is no hosel. These are mostly aesthetic concerns.

Grips
Grips are different, too. Most putter grips are larger than those on your other clubs. This helps promote a lighter grip pressure and prevents the wrists from breaking too easily.

NOTE: New Ladies Putters enter the market all the time, so please make sure you visit http://bit.ly/LadyGolfersGuide on a regular basis. There we will introduce you to the newest clubs and trends.

Golf Balls

Golf's biggest advancements have come via dramatic improvements in ball construction. Compared to 30 years ago, today's golf ball travels farther, rolls longer, doesn't lose its round, flies straighter, and won't split its cover if you look at it wrong. Precisely engineered dimple patterns have allowed manufacturers to alter everything from trajectory to spin rates. As a result of these breakthroughs, players now have the opportunity to choose and play the best ball for their games.

Years ago, everyone played with a soft, easy-cutting, natural rubber, balata-covered ball-- whether you were a scratch player or a 25 handicap. Today, you're lucky to have numerous choices. However, options don't necessarily make things easier. In fact, finding the right ball for your game can be confusing. Rather than have you spend hours researching your options, we did it for you. But first some background info:

Golf Ball Specifics

In order to provide a fair game, the golf ball must be standardized. This standard is set by the United States Golf Association (USGA) for the United States and Mexico, and the R&A (taken from the Royal and Ancient Golf Club of St Andrews) for the rest of the world.

Each golf ball must pass the following requirements to be considered legal:

- **Weight** – The golf ball must not weigh more than 1.620 ounces (45.93gm). There is no minimum weight.

- **Size** – The diameter of the golf ball must not be smaller than 1.680 inches (42.67mm). There is no maximum size.

- **Spherical Symmetry** – The golf ball must be symmetrical in shape.

- **Initial Velocity** – The golf ball must not exceed a certain initial takeoff speed.

- **Overall Distance Standard** – The golf ball must not exceed a certain overall distance, including roll.

What do the Numbers on a Golf Ball mean?

Most golfers just look at the name brand of the golf ball they're using. They only look at a golf ball's number when attempting to identify it from another.

However, the numbers exist for more than mere identification:

- **Single-Digit** – A single digit on a golf ball is mainly used for identification purposes. The numbers generally range from 1 to 4.

- **70-200** – A number ranging from 70-200 indicates the compression rating. Compression relates to the hardness of a golf ball. The higher the number, the harder the ball (please see below for more on compression). The most common compression range is 90 to 100. Unfortunately, this number is not standardized.

- **300-400** – A ball with a number ranging from 300 to 400 indicates the number of dimples on the ball.

The golf ball underwent a dramatic change in recent years. In 1996, the multilayered ball was created to assist golfers striving for more distance. The Top-Flite Strata was the first multilayer ball to be produced. This ball introduced a hard mantle to bridge the gap between the solid core and the cover. This so-called mantle helps to reduce the spin created by the driver. According to the manufacturer, this reduces the height and increases the distance.

At turn of the century, another distance ball was born. The Titleist Pro V1 featured a solid core and polyurethane cover. According to Golf Digest, this ball outdistanced the others by more than 6 yards.

Every golfer's dream is to hit the ball farther and farther. In order to do so, golfers seek the highest quality of balls on the market. However, this comes at a price: these top golf balls cost a small fortune each. If you hit them in the water hazard it's like throwing money into the pond.

The current top of the line balls require a high level of skill to achieve the desired distance. Unfortunately, most golfers who purchase these balls don't have the necessary skill but think they can get it by purchasing these expensive balls.

Ball Types

There are two main classes of balls: spin and distance.

Spin: Designed to spin more. Often, they are of three-piece construction. A central core (liquid in the highest spin balls) is surrounded by rubber windings, which is often covered with a thin, soft material called balata. These balls spin more, making them easier to draw or fade, and they hold the green. They also have a softer feel but won't travel as far as distance balls. Less expensive versions of these balls offer a measure of durability. Their cover is typically Surlyn (a durable, synthetic material) or a Surlyn blend, they may be two-piece rather than three-piece, and have a solid core.

Distance: Made with harder, more-durable covers and solid cores. Most are two piece. The inside of the distance ball is a firm synthetic material. The combined firmness of the cover and core allow the ball to travel longer distances and be very durable. However, these balls don't spin a great amount. Less spin means less control and stopping ability in certain cases. These have a harder feel than balls with wound construction.

Covers: Balata vs. Surlyn

Balata and Surlyn are popular ball-covering materials. However, there are typically other differences between balata and surlyn balls besides just the cover:

Surlyn
A surlyn covered ball is typically a two-piece ball: a solid core with the surlyn cover. Surlyn is a man made "uncuttable" substance which is designed to eliminate the cuts and nicks. The drawbacks of the harder ball are that it is more difficult to "shape" his/her shot *(fade/draw)*, and get "action" *(backspin)* on the greens.

Typical 3-piece wound ball

Balata
A balata covered ball is typically a three-piece ball: a core wound with rubber and covered with balata. There has been a lot of discussion as to what "balata" is. Let's just say that balata is a soft substance which leads to cuts and nicks. This "softness" is said to offer "better playability" which is to say that the golfer can "shape" his/her shot *(fade/draw)*, and get more "action" *(backspin)* on the greens. Most Lady Golfers prefer Balata balls over Surlyn as it benefits their slower swing speed.

Balata	**Surlyn**
Softer cover	Harder cover
Better spin	Not as much spin
Scuffs and cuts easily	Resists scuffs and cuts
"Works" the ball better because of spin *(Draw, fade, backspin)*	More distance
Usually three-piece ball *(Liquid-filled core, wound rubber, and cover)*	Usually two-piece ball *(Solid core and cover)*
Usually more expensive:	Usually less expensive:
- Higher first cost	- Lower first cost
- Shorter life	- Longer life

Compression

Golf ball manufacturers use compression machines to measure how much their balls will deform under a certain weight. The lower the compression rate, the more the ball can be compressed. This produces a softer the ball that will give the player .more feel. Unfortunately, not all machines used to measure compression are equal. Consequently, different manufacturers may indicate different numbers for the same ball. The compression rate may also be shown on a ball.

Lady Golfers with average swing speeds should use Compression 80. Temperature also affects the performance of the ball. Warm temperature has a positive effect on high compression balls, whereas cool temperature has the same effect on low compression balls.

Putting

All balls behave differently. This behavior is apparent on the putting green. Harder balls roll farther than softer balls. The difference in distance may surprise you. Professional instructors always advise their students to putt with the same type of ball. This will enable beginners to develop feel and calibrate the distance of their putting strokes.

No golf ball is perfect. In fact, most balls aren't well balanced and don't always roll the same way during a putt. Next time you miss a 4-foot putt, blame it on the ball. Premium balls are subject to higher quality control and less likely to drift.

NOTE: New Ladies Golf Balls enter the market all the time, so please make sure you visit http://bit.ly/LadyGolfersGuide on a regular basis. There we will introduce you to the newest clubs and trends.

Purchasing Golf Equipment – what to look out for

We women are just as interested in scoring well as men are, too. That's why ladies should be concerned with buying the proper equipment, since proper equipment can make a huge difference on the scorecard. Golf clubs manufacturers have taken notice recently of this huge interest in their women's equipment, and they have responded with a lot more selection and quality. Today's women's equipment is lightweight, easier to control, and set at the proper lengths to match all skill levels, personal tastes, and body types.

For instance, many women's woods come with variable length lines that allow women of varying hits to accurately hit them. If a women's wood doesn't specifically mention its height requirements that means it can work for women who are five foot five to five foot nine.

Such flexible woods are crucial for many women players, since they use woods more often than irons, even in the fairway. Woods tend to give women bigger "sweet spots," or hitting areas, compared to irons. The bottoms of fairway woods are made so they glide without friction over the ground. And the length of these woods usually is greater than the length of comparable irons, say a 4 wood compared to a 6 iron. For a women, this all means that woods are easier to hit, more likely to launch a ball straight into the air, and hit farther than irons.

For the short game, look for golf clubs that feel comfortable in your swing, feel light, and short enough for you to get underneath the ball. An 8 and 9 iron, or pitching wedge, can come in handy when you have a short approach shot that requires precision rather than distance. Once you land on the green, pull out the proper putter. If you're shorter than five foot five, that means a putter shorter than 33 inches in length. If you're taller than that, tinker with putters in the store until you find one that's comfortable.

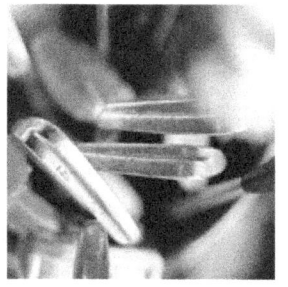

We all want to improve our game-whether you're a beginner, an intermediate, or a highly skilled player. The better you are, the more you enjoy playing. While practice is the key to improving, other factors sometimes impede your progress, like your clubs. Having the right clubs increases your chance of playing well and instils self-confidence-a critical factor in improving your game.

But finding the right clubs is a challenge. With so many options out there, it's hard to know which ones are right for you. Our buyers guide provides information that will help you choose the right clubs for you. Easy to understand, the guide offers a step-by-step approach for selecting the right clubs.

When it comes to buying equipment, we all think alike: The higher the price, the better the clubs. While price often indicates quality, those expensive brand name clubs touted by a PGA pro may not be right for you. You don't need a $1200 set of clubs to play well. In fact, you can play better with clubs costing hundreds less than brand names if they fit your swing and your game. How do you find the right clubs?

Knowledge is the key to selecting your clubs. Knowing how a club affects your swing and your ball striking helps you choose a set that's right for you. That's something only you can do. Your favourite salesman at the local pro shop-as knowledgeable as he is about clubs-can provide some help, but it's limited, since he probably doesn't know how you play. Using our guide will help you make a better, more informed decision.

The major components of a golf club are the head, the shaft, and the grip. These components come in a variety of makes, models, sizes, and materials. If one of these components doesn't match your swing or if your clubs are too old, you'll struggle to improve your game. Below are details on these key components.

Club Head Style

Manufacturers have come a long way in club making technology. Today, clubs are more forgiving than ever, and no where is the impact of those advances felt more than in club head design and construction. A club head's main characteristics are offset, perimeter weighting, sole width, heel-to-toe length, and face height.

Offset

Offset is the amount the face of a club sits back from the hosel of the club. Offset reduces the chances of hitting a slice and increases the chances making solid contact with the ball. Solid contact affects distance and accuracy. Better golfers require less offset than poorer players. In fact, offset can be a major factor in helping players with high handicaps play well. Even players with lower handicaps benefit from using clubs with offset club heads.

Perimeter Weighting

Perimeter weighting places more material around the club head's perimeter than its center, creating a larger sweet spot on the club. This design makes the club more forgiving when hit and reduces the effects of miss-hits. Better players prefer the club head's mass behind the center to achieve more distance. Poorer players want the weight around the perimeter to correct off-center hits. If you're a highly skilled player, buy clubs with no perimeter weighting. If you are a less skilled player, opt for clubs with perimeter weighting.

Size

Size is another factor when buying irons. Put simply, the larger the club head, the easier it is to get entangled in the rough or a plush lie. The smaller the sole, the easier it is to get out of the rough or a plush lie. That's why many teaching pros recommend a mid- to wide-soled iron for clubs from 2 to 9, and more blade style irons for wedges. Blade style clubs improve your chances of hitting out of the rough or a plush lie while providing the ability to stop the ball quickly on the green. Consider buying blade style wedges if you often find yourself playing from the rough.

Heel-to-Toe Length

Heel-to-toe length is more cosmetic then anything else, although it somewhat affects forgiveness. Some players simply like the look of a more compact iron even though the longer heel-to-toe design offers a larger, more effective hitting area. If you want the maximum amount of forgiveness in your clubs, select ones with a longer heel-to-toe design.

Face Height

Face height is similar to heel-to-toe length. If you are looking for the most forgiving irons you can find, choose ones that have more face height.

Shafts

Poor ball flight pattern plagues many golfers. Poor pattern causes players to lose 3-5 strokes or more a round. The ideal is a high, penetrating shot that lands softly on the green or the fairway. Too low a ball flight pattern prevents you from stopping your shot where you want. Instead, the ball rolls off the green into trouble. Too high a ball flight pattern robs you of distance, preventing you from clearing hazards or from reaching the green on an approach shot. Poor ball flight pattern could be a sign that you don't have the right shaft for your clubs.

The shaft is a vital consideration when buying clubs. The key features of a shaft are flex, torque, length, and weight. If one of these features is off, it affects your swing, preventing your ball from achieving that high, penetrating shot we all want. Below is information on each of the key features of a shaft.

Flex

Flex is one of the most important, if not the most important, feature when selecting a shaft. Flex is the amount a club bends during the swing. The shaft's flex must match the player's swing speed for best results. If there's too much flex, the player has less control of the ball when hit. This player will have a tendency to draw or hook the ball. It there's not enough flex, the player loses distance but gains control. This player will have a tendency to fade or slice the ball. For Lady Golfers the recommended flex is 'L'.

Torque

Another important consideration is torque. Torque is the amount the club head twists when the player swings the club. Torque, like flex, must match the player's swing speed. To get the maximum distance and control from a shaft, you need to have the right torque rating. If you have a shaft with a rating of 2.5 stiff and you're hitting the ball 200 yards without roll, you're probably not getting the most out of your shaft. That's because you're not putting enough load on the shaft to maximize the club's torque rating. Without sufficient load, the shaft won't unload at its maximum capability.

Many players need help getting the clubhead to release properly through impact. That's where torque comes in. More torque, however, means less control of the club head when hitting the ball.

Shaft Weight

Weight affects how the club feels. Every golfer likes a different feel to his clubs. Some like clubs with their weight in the club head, others like clubs with their weight more evenly distributed. Some like irons with the weight in the club head, and woods with the weight evenly distributed. Others like irons with the weight evenly distributed and woods with the weight in the club head. It all depends on the feel. The feel of a club is important because it affects the player psychologically. That, in turn, affects his self-confidence.

Shaft Length

Do you often find yourself choking up on your clubs? Does your back hurt the morning after a round of golf? That's your body telling you your clubs are too long or too short. Your body changes its motion to compensate for the wrong size clubs. Using a new motion brings new muscles into play, stressing them and generating pain. This change also hampers your swing rhythm, a key to playing successful golf. Without good rhythm, the player will never develop a powerful swing.

If your clubs are too long, you'll see these types of shots:

- Low Hook
- Higher ball flight
- Fat shots
- Worm burners
- Push or Slice

Low Hook - The extra long shaft makes the club's toe stick up, causing the heel to grab the ball first. This development in turn creates right to left spin on the ball and lower ball flight.

Higher Ball Flight - Golfers often compensate for the additional length by standing too tall and leaning back on their downswing. Leaning back creates extra loft, causing a high shot with little distance.

Fat Shots - Because you have longer shafts you tend to compensate for the additional shaft length. But you forget to compensate about 40 percent of the time. This causes you to make contact with the ground a hair to soon, resulting in fat shots.

Worm Burner - This is the opposite of the fat shot. Here, you over compensate for shaft length by standing too tall. Instead of making solid contact with the ball, you hit the upper part of the ball, causing a worm burner or the low skimming shot that flies 60 yards over the green.

If your clubs are too short, you'll see these types of shots:

- Push or slice
- Catch the ball thin

Push or Slice - An iron that's too short points the toe into the ground, causing it to grab the ball too early in the swing. It also pushes your heel forward, which in turn generates left to right spin on the ball resulting in a push or a slice.

Catching It Thin - If you're hitting weak shots with little distance or height, you may be simply catching the ball too thin. That's a clear indication that the clubs are too short for you.

Graphite or Steel shafts?

It used to be that recreational golfers and those with a mid- and high-handicap would stick with the graphite while the more advanced players and low-handicappers would switch to steel. But times change and so did that mindset. Most pros have made the move from steel to graphite in recent years and in 2004 Tiger Woods joined them, switching to a graphite shaft in his driver.

When deciding whether or not you wish to make the switch from steel to graphite - or vice versa - there are some key differences between the two that you should note:

Key points

- Steel shafts are less expensive than graphite, meaning the cost of a steel set of clubs is substantially less than a graphite set of clubs.
- Graphite shafts are now as durable as steel shafts, though both have their weak points. Quality graphite shafts last a long time so long as they are not chipped or cracked, or the laminate-seal is not peeling. Steel shafts will last forever so long as they are not bent, rusted or pitted.
- You get less vibration in your hands with graphite shafts, and more vibrations with steel shafts. It depends on how much vibrations you want. Some amateurs like the extra feedback that steel provides while many prefer as little vibration as possible. If you are prone to a lot of bad hits, your hands might be buzzing after a round with a steel shaft.
- Most important is the weight difference. Graphite shafts, and therefore graphite clubs, are much lighter than steel shafts and steel clubs.

In the ever-lasting quest to gain even precious yardage on their swing, many golfers have made the switch from steel to graphite. According to club-making and equipment guru Tom Wishon, you can gain an extra 6-12 yards of distance on your drive with graphite.

Before you say "Well that's it then, I'm switching to graphite" there are some other points you will want to consider:

Steel shafts are still very much a part of the great game of golf. Many players, namely low-handicappers and scratch players even prefer them. So do those big swingers who feel they don't need extra distance in their swing that a graphite shaft can provide. Many feel that a steel shaft gives them better control over their club head. Others like the added feedback (as we discussed) that comes from more vibrations up and down the shaft on a bad shot.

Tom Wishon himself says this: "If gaining more distance is a primary goal for the golfer, they should definitely be fit with the proper graphite shaft design in their woods and irons to match their swing. On the other hand, if distance is not the main focus for the golfer because they already have a high swing speed, if they like the feel of steel and their swing tempo matches a little better to the higher total weight steel shafts bring to the clubs, then steel is the better option."

It may be said that steel shafts are for steely players, those who are physically strong and have no problems in their hands, forearms or shoulders. Everyone else may want to go with graphite. There is no shame in making the choice because that's the way the majority go these days.

Should you buy brand name Clubs?

One decision facing today's golfers is whether to buy expensive brand name clubs or less-expensive clones. Both offer superior performance and world-class quality, but the clones are a better value. While the decision to buy cloned clubs rests with the golfer, it's not an easy one. It helps to have some basic information about cloned clubs before buying.

Golf club manufacturing is dominated by a few select firms. Callaway®, Titleist®, TaylorMade® and Cobra® are among the game's finest manufacturers. These firms stay abreast of the latest technological developments to provide the best clubs available.

Always striving to introduce the latest innovations, these firms compete fiercely with each other in a hotly contested marketplace. When one introduces an innovative club, the others quickly follow suit.

For example, Callaway®, TaylorMade®, Titleist® and Cobra® all market a metal driver with a graphite shaft. Each model features an oversize club head, a deeper clubface, and a low center of gravity. Each boasts of providing ultimate distance, forgiveness, and accuracy. And each claims to offer reduced spin.

Manufacturers of brand name clubs spend millions promoting their clubs. The money for promotional activities is included in the cost of manufacturing the clubs. Golf Digest estimates that a $500 driver actually costs about $77 to produce ($55 for the club head, $15 for a graphite shaft, $3 for the grip, and $4 for assembly). The remaining $423 covers overhead and other expenses as well as promotional activities. The more a company spends on promotion, the higher the cost of producing the clubs. The manufacturer passes the additional costs on to consumers in the form of higher prices.

A great alternative are Clone Golf Clubs. Clones provide a reference to a style and are not copy cat clubs or knock-offs. Clone sold by reputable merchants are all legal designs that do not infringe the rights of other golf equipment manufacturers. Clones offer a better value, as they are manufactured from similar materials utilizing similar features to the name brands, but cost far less. They provide the same performance, quality, and technological features as brand name clubs but are more cost-effectively. Golfers save between 50 percent and 75 percent of the name brand's retail price. The saving equates to about several hundred dollars for a set of clubs. Lower prices let you buy new clubs more often, while enabling you to stay abreast of the newest designs and latest features.

Clones are every bit as good as name brand clubs. Clones are manufactured from the same components as the originals. Clone manufacturers buy their club heads, shafts, and grips from the same small community of suppliers as name brand companies. Clone manufacturers offer a wide range of shaft and grip options just like the original manufacturers. And clone manufacturers offer the same make of grips and shafts as name brand companies. The difference in playability between a brand name club and a good clone is generally insignificant. Clone manufacturer's prices are lower because they don't market their clubs as aggressively as name brand companies, eliminating most promotional expenses.

Legitimate clone manufacturers uphold the rights of name brand manufacturers. They clearly state their company's name on their product, and make no attempt to mislead customers on the manufacturer. Legitimate clone manufacturers also uphold the legal trademarks, patents, and copyrights of other companies. Based on my own experience I strongly suggest that you take a look at the selections at golf clone manufacturers her: http://bit.ly/LadyGolfersGuide. The quality of the clubs shown there is comparable to well known brands, but their prices are way more 'realistic'.

But some 'black sheep' manufacturers that violate these copy rights. Clubs that bear close resemblance to a name brand club lead the consumer to believe they are manufactured by an original manufacturer, or are exact copies of a brand name club. These clubs are illegal. They should not be purchased.

Manufacturers of illegal clones offer inferior quality, durability, and performance. Some use a poorer grade of stainless steel in their shafts and club heads, which quickly rust when exposed to dampness. Others use inferior titanium alloys, which include adding significantly more aluminum than titanium. Still others use inferior paint, which wears off almost immediately. What's more, shafts are often inferior factory seconds that have been painted to look like high quality shafts. Regardless of how they do it, illegal clone manufacturers are just trying to rip you off.

Golfers need to be aware of illegal clubs and counterfeit products when purchasing equipment. If you decide to buy clone golf clubs, research the manufacturer thoroughly before buying them. Illegal clones produced by disreputable manufacturers are readily available. If a company's name can't be identified on a club, it's probably illegal and most likely of inferior quality. Be weary of them.

Buying used Golf Clubs

Used clubs are a good alternative if you're on a budget. Sometimes you can find a great deal in used clubs. Many golfers like to test the latest equipment on the market. These are usually high-handicapped golfers with plenty of money to burn. What they want is to show off their gleaming new golf sets. To them 'Golf is for show'. These golfers would never be caught using sets more than a year old and they will gladly sell them to you cheaply. If you happen to know any such golfers, consider yourself lucky.

You may also find used sets which are quite suitable to your play. It's preferable to purchase a used set that suits you than to invest in a new set that isn't suitable. You can often get a well priced set advertised at your local driving range or in your newspapers classifieds. Don't buy the clubs blindly; take a close look at them first. In particular check the following:

Clubheads

Check for clubface wear. See whether there is a marked difference in the metal. If the center of the clubface is shinier, it's a good indication the club has been well used. Also check for grooves. Do they have well defined edges? If the center grooves are shallower than the rest, the clubhead has been worn down.

Examine the face at eye level. Do you notice a smooth surface or one with indentations? Avoid clubs with an irregular surface. You won't hit consistently.

Shafts
Any indentation on a shaft indicates a serious weakness. That part of the shaft has hit a hard object such as a tree, signpost, marker stakes or another club.
Scratches are often found near the hosel. They are usually caused by the clubhead of an adjacent club in the bag. This is an indication that the previous owner didn't take care of his clubs.

For graphite shafts, test the torque by twisting it in opposite directions. If it twists, it's useful life is over.

Some steel shafts have been bent back into shape. Look down the shaft to see this imperfection. Sometimes you can feel it.

Check for rust. Small specks or faint dots all over indicate the shaft has been polished to remove the rust spots.

Are all the shafts of the same make? A different shaft gives a different feel.

Grips
Expect some reasonable wear and tear. Check for cracks and tears. If you need to re-grip the whole set of clubs, a set isn't worth buying.

Set Consistency
Line up the clubs in order; there should be a half inch difference between each pair. Do they appear to come from the original set? Non-homogeneous clubs may not have a uniform progression of lofts throughout the set.

Check Current Prices
Find out the price of the equivalent new set of the model you're buying. Don't be surprised if there is little price difference, especially if the model has been discontinued by the manufacturer. You can use this info when haggling with the seller.

Try Them Out
Ask the seller to meet you at the local driving range, there you can try to hit a few balls and see if you are comfortable.

Care & Maintenance of Clubs

Since you have invested in a set of golf clubs, you should keep them in good condition. Take good care of them, and they'll take good care of your scores.

Here are some tips on the maintenance and care of golf clubs:

- It's hard to return from a round without your clubs getting dirty. Mud, sand, or squashed grass will adhere to the grooves on your clubheads. This will affect the flight of the golf ball. Use a wet towel to wipe mud off the clubhead and use a brush to clean the grooves. Don't use metal objects such as a metal brush or nails.

- After a round, wash the clubs with water and wipe them dry with a cloth. If you have time, spread the clubs out to dry before putting them back in your bag.

- At home, soak your clubheads in a pail of soapy water. Clean the grooves of your clubs with a stiff fiber of plastic brush. Don't use a metal brush.

- Grips need to be replaced after some time. Check if the dimples remain. If not, its time to change grip.

- Re-gripping a club is not difficult if you know how to do it. You can buy a re-gripping package with detailed instructions on how to re-grip a club.

Besides prolonging the lifespan of your golf set, having a well-cared set also projects a positive image.

What to look for in Golf Shoes

A good pair of golf shoes is an important component in a round of golf just like properly fitted clubs and the right golf balls. Particularly by beginner golfers golf shoes are often considered as 'just a fashion accessory', selected solely on the basis of design and price. However, it is very important to consider how the proper, or improper, combination of foot type and golf shoe type affects ones game in terms of comfort, performance and stamina.

Let's face it - it is your feet that provide the foundation for your body - and ultimately your swing. Your timing, distance and direction are based, amongst many other parameters, on a controlled lower body movement. With the feet leading the way any problems with proper ground contact will not only impede timing and balance but also your score. Fortunately the abundance of different brands, models and designs available on the market makes it possible to improve your game with better-fitting shoes.

Among the popular golf shoe brands are (in alphabetical order) Bite, Calloway Golf, Ecco, Etonic, FootJoy and Nike Golf. All of these brands have golf shoe sizes available for ladies, usually also in narrow and wide width specialty sizes.

Just to mention a few recent golf shoe developments:

FootJoy offers a spikeless golf shoe (pictured right) with comfortable insoles name Slip Last Construction. This unique construction produces a more contoured underfoot platform and increased flexibility because the shoe is made without an insole board.

Adidas has developed a torsion system for their shoes which is designed to stabilize the natural motion which occurs from your feet thru the legs during each golf swing. This patented torsion system helps to control excess movement and maintains stability. Of course the competition for comfort is great as well, so Adidas makes an added cushion in the heel area to protect the foot from discomfort during repetitive impact.

Spikeless Golf Shoe

There are a lot of variations in golf shoes, so it really depends on the kind of game you play and the features you will want. A good start is to look for features such as rubber spikes or removable cleats, waterproof construction, and breathable material. If your shoes are not waterproof you should apply a waterproofing spray, otherwise your feet will get wet when walking thru moist grass. In addition shoes should provide an air cushioned insole or another form of comfort fit. Since you walk for hours at a time it is very important to stay comfortable, and to limit moisture build up inside the shoe.

Ladies golf shoes are more expensive in retail stores than online, but at least you get to try them on. Some shoppers try out their golf shoes in a retail shop but order the same pair online to save some money.

NOTE: New Ladies Golf Shoes come into the market all the time, so please make sure you visit **http://bit.ly/LadyGolfersGuide** on a regular basis. There we will introduce you to the newest trends.

Basic Rules of the Game

You must learn the rules when you play golf. Few golfers know every single rule, not even the pros. However, it's imperative that you are familiar with the common rules. Otherwise, you will be a burden to your golf partners.

Knowing the rules puts you in an advantageous position over a person who doesn't know them. You will know that it's legal to clean your ball when it's on the green. You will also realize that you can pull out an embedded ball without incurring a penalty.

The rules of golf are internationally standardized and are jointly governed by the Royal and Ancient Golf Club of St Andrews (R&A) and the United States Golf Association (USGA). By agreement with the R&A, the USGA jurisdiction on the enforcement and interpretation of the rules is limited to the United States and Mexico, while the R&A covers the rest of the world. The rules continue to evolve; amended versions of the rule book are usually published and made effective in a four-year cycle, the latest being from 2008 to 2011.

The underlying principle of the rules is fairness. As declared on the back cover of the official rule book: "Play the ball as it lies, play the course as you find it, and if you can't do either, do what is fair."

Decisions on the Rules of Golf are based on formal case decisions by the R&A and USGA and are published regularly.

The etiquette of golf, although not formally equivalent to the rules, are included in the publications on golf rules and are considered binding for every player. They cover matters such as safety, fairness, easiness and pace of play, and players' obligation to contribute to the care of the course.

There are strict regulations regarding the amateur status of golfers. Essentially, everybody who has ever taught or played golf for money (or even accepted a trophy of more than a modest monetary value) is not considered an amateur and must not participate in amateur competitions. this also applies to hole-in-one prizes: if the monetary value of the prize exceeds the equivalent of 500 British Pounds an amateur can not accept it without loosing his/her amateur status.

The following section mentions the most important ones, try to learn them before your next game.

Rule 1 -- The Game

The holes on the course must be played in order (1 through 9, 10 through 18 or 1 through 18).

You must always play by the Rules. You are not allowed to change them.

Rule 2 -- Match Play

In match play, each hole is a separate contest. If you win the first hole, you are "one-up"; if you lose it, you are "one-down"; if you tie it, you are "all-square."

You have won the match when, for example, you are three-up and there are only two holes left to play.

Anyone you are playing against is your "opponent."

Rule 3 -- Stroke Play

In stroke play, the competitor with the lowest total score for the round (9 or 18 holes) is the winner.

You must play the ball into the hole before starting the next hole.

Anyone you are playing with is a fellow-competitor.

Rules 4 & 5 -- Clubs and the Ball

You may carry no more than fourteen clubs.

Normally, you may not change balls during the play of a hole. However, if you damage or cut your ball, you may change the ball after first asking your opponent or fellow competitor.

Rule 6 -- Things a Player Should Do

Read the notices given to you by the tournament officials.

Always use your proper handicap.

Know your tee-time or starting time.

Make sure you play your own ball (put a mark on the ball in case someone else is using an identical ball.

In stroke play, make sure your score for each hole is correct before you turn in your card.

Keep playing unless there is lightning, you are ill or an official tells you to stop.

Rule 7 -- Practice

You may not hit a practice shot while playing a hole, or from any hazard.
Note: Always read the local rules about practice.

Rule 8 -- Advice on How to Play

During a round, you may not ask anyone except your caddie or partner for advice on how to play. However, you may ask about Rules or the position of hazards or the flagstick.

You may not give advice to your opponent or fellow-competitor

Rule 9 -- Advising Opponent on Strokes Taken

In match play, you must tell your opponent the number of strokes you have taken if you are asked.

Rule 10 -- When to Play a Shot

The player who has the lowest score on a hole has the right to play his/her ball first on the next hole. This is called the "honor."

While playing a hole, the player whose ball is farthest from the hole plays first.

In match play, if you play out of turn, your opponent may make you replay your shot. This is not so in stroke play.

Rule 11 -- Teeing Ground

Tee your ball between the tee-markers or a little behind them. You may tee your ball as far as two club lengths behind the markers.

If your ball accidentally falls off the tee, you may replace it without penalty.

Rule 12 -- Finding Ball in Hazard -- Identifying Ball

A hazard is any bunker (area of sand) or water hazard (lake, pond, creek, etc).

In a bunker or water hazard, if sand or leaves cover your ball, you may remove enough of the sand or leaves to be able to see a part of the ball.

You may lift your ball to identify it anywhere except in a hazard [Note: this rule will change from January 1, 2008: you will be allowed to lift your ball in a hazard for identification purposes]. You must tell your opponent or fellow competitor before you lift your ball to identify it.

Rule 13 -- Playing the Ball as it Lies on the Course

You must play the ball as it lies. You may not move it to a better spot.

You may not improve your lie by pressing down behind the ball. The club may be grounded only lightly behind the ball.

You may not improve the area of your intended swing or line of play by bending or breaking anything growing, such as tree limbs or weeds.

In a hazard, you may not touch the sand, ground or water with the club before or during your back swing.

In a hazard, you may not remove loose impediments (natural things such as leaves or twigs) but you may remove obstructions (artificial objects such as bottles or rakes.)

Rule 14 -- Striking the Ball

You must strike the ball fairly with the head of the club. You may not push, scrape or rake the ball.

You must not hit your ball while it is moving.

Rule 15 -- Playing a Wrong Ball

In match play, if you play a ball that is not yours, you lose the hole. If you play the wrong ball in a hazard, there is no penalty and you must then play the right ball (see note below).

In stroke play, if you play a ball that is not yours, you must take a two-stroke penalty. If you play the wrong ball in a hazard, you must then play out the hole with your own ball. If you do not do so, you are disqualified.

[**Note:** this rule will change from January 1, 2008: since you will be allowed to lift the ball in a hazard for identification purposes you will incur the same penalty for playing the wrong ball outside the hazard if you play the wrong ball from inside the hazard.]

Rule 16 -- The Putting Green

If any part of your ball is touching the green, it is on the green.

When your ball is on the green, you may brush away leaves and other loose impediments within your line of putt with your hand or a club. Do not fan them with a cap or towel.

You should repair ball marks or old hole plugs if they are within your line of putt, but you may not repair marks made by spikes or shoes.

You may not test the surface of the green by rolling a ball or scraping the surface.

Always mark your ball by putting a small coin or other marker behind it when you want to pick it up to clean or get it out of another player's way.

Rule 17 -- The Flagstick

If your ball is off the green, there is no penalty if you play and your ball strikes the flagstick, provided no one is holding the flagstick.

If your ball is on the green, do not putt with the flagstick in the hole. Either take the flagstick out or ask another player to hold it and take it out when you play your ball. In match play, if you putt and your ball hits the flagstick when it is in the hole, you lose the hole. In stroke play, you must add two penalty strokes to your score for the hole.

Rule 18 -- Moving the Ball

If you or your partner move either of your balls on purpose or accidentally, add a penalty stroke to your score, replace and play it.

If someone or something moves your ball other than you or your partner, (an outside agency) there is no penalty, but you must replace it. If the ball is moved by wind or water, you must play it as it lies.

Once you address the ball, if the ball moves, add a penalty stroke and replace the ball.

If you move a loose impediment lying within one club-length of the ball and the ball moves, add a penalty stroke, replace it and play it. On the putting green, there is no penalty.

Rule 19 -- Ball in Motion Deflected or Stopped

If your ball hits an outside agency, (bird, rake, etc.), it is called a "rub of the green." There is no penalty and the ball is played as it lies.

"Rub of the green." Play the ball as it lies. No penalty.

If your ball hits you, your partner, your caddie, or your equipment in match play you lose the hole. In stroke play, you are penalized two strokes and you must play your ball as it lies.

[Note: from 1 January 2008 the penalty will be reduced to 1 stroke for both match play and stroke play].

If your ball hits your opponent, his caddie, or his equipment, there is no penalty; you may play the ball as it lies or replay the shot.

If your ball hits a fellow competitor, caddie or equipment in stroke play, there is no penalty and the ball is played as it lies. These are the same as outside agencies in stroke play.

If your ball hits another ball and moves it, you must play your ball as it lies. The owner of the other ball must replace it. If your ball is on the green when you play and the ball, which your ball hits, is also on the green, you are penalized two strokes in stroke play. Otherwise, there is no penalty.

Rule 20 -- Lifting and Dropping the Ball

If you are going to lift your ball under a Rule and the Rule requires that the ball be replaced, you must put a ball-marker behind the ball before you lift it.

When you drop a ball, stand erect, hold your arm out straight and drop it.

If a dropped ball hits the ground and rolls into a hazard, out of a hazard, comes to rest more than two club-lengths from where it first struck a part of the course, nearer the hole or, if you are dropping away from an immovable obstruction or ground under repair, etc., back into the obstruction or ground under repair, you must re-drop. If the same thing happens when you re-drop, you must place the ball where it struck the ground when it was re-dropped.

Rule 21 -- Cleaning the Ball

You may clean your ball when you are allowed to lift it. On the green a ball may be cleaned when lifted except when it has been lifted to determine if it is unfit or for identification purposes because it interferes with play.

Rule 22 -- Ball Interfering with or Assisting Play

If another ball interferes with your swing or is in your line of putt, you may ask the owner of the ball to lift it.

If your ball is near the hole and might serve as a backstop for another player, you may lift your ball.

Rule 23 -- Loose Impediments

Loose impediments are natural objects that are not growing or fixed -- such as leaves, twigs, branches, worms and insects. You may remove a loose impediment except when your ball and the loose impediment lie in a bunker or water hazard. (Exception see Rule 12)

Rule 24 -- Obstructions

Obstructions are artificial or man-made objects. Bottles, tin cans, rakes, etc., are movable obstructions. Sprinkler heads, shelter houses, cart paths, etc., are Immovable obstructions.

Movable obstructions anywhere on the course may be removed. If the ball moves when moving an obstruction, it must be replaced without penalty.

You may drop your ball away from an immovable obstruction if it interferes with your swing or stance. Find the nearest point not nearer the hole where you can play without interference with your swing or stance. Drop the ball within one club-length of that point. (You may move your ball away from an immovable obstruction if it interferes with your swing or stance.) Note: You should not pick up the ball from an obstruction until you have established the nearest point of relief.

[Note: from January 1, 2008 you will be allowed to move the flag stick when the ball is in motion.]

Rule 25 -- Casual Water; Ground Under Repair; Animal Holes

Casual water is any temporary puddle of water caused by rain or over watering. Ground under repair is any damaged area, which the Committee has marked as such.

If your ball or your stance is in casual water, ground under repair or a burrowing animal hole, you may either play the ball as it lies or find the nearest place not nearer the hole which gives you relief, and drop the ball within one club-length of that place.

If your ball is in casual water, etc., and you cannot find it, determine where the ball entered the area and drop a ball within one club-length of that place without penalty.

If your ball is on the wrong green, find the nearest place off the green, which is not nearer the hole, and drop the ball within one club-length of that place.

Rule 26 -- Water Hazards

Water hazard margins are identified by yellow stakes or lines. Lateral water hazard margins are identified by red stakes or lines.

If your ball is in a water hazard or a lateral water hazard, you may play it as it lies. If you cannot find it or do not wish to play it, add a penalty stroke and drop and play another ball from where you last played; or drop a ball behind the water hazard as far back as you wish. If you decide to drop behind the hazard, drop the ball so that there is a straight line between the hole, where your ball last crossed the hazard margin and where you drop the ball. If your ball is in a lateral water hazard, you may drop a ball within two club-lengths of where the ball last crossed the hazard margin, no nearer to the hole.

Rule 27 -- Ball Lost or Out of Bounds

A ball is lost if it is not found within five minutes after you first begin to search.

A ball is out of bounds when all of it lies beyond the inside line of objects such as white stakes, or a fence or wall that marks the playing area.

If your ball is lost or out of bounds, you must add a penalty stroke to your score and play another ball from where you played your last shot.

If you think your ball may be lost or out of bounds, you may play another ball (provisional ball) from the place where your first ball was played. You must tell your opponent or fellow-competitor that you are playing a provisional ball and play it before you look for the first ball. If you cannot find your first ball or if it is out of bounds, you must count the strokes with the first and provisional balls, add a penalty stroke and play out the hole with the provisional ball. If you find your first ball in bounds, continue play with it and pick up the provisional ball.

Rule 28 -- Ball Unplayable

If your ball is under a tree or in some other bad situation and you decide you cannot play it, add a penalty stroke and do one of the following:

1. Go back to where you played the last shot and play a ball from there

2. Measure two club-lengths from the unplayable lie, drop a ball and play from there

3. Keep the unplayable lie between where you may drop the ball and the hole, go back as far as you wish on a straight line and drop and play the ball.

Golf How To's

In this section we look at some frequently asked questions:

How to mark a Scorecard

All golf courses provide scorecards so you can keep track of each player's score. Players count all the strokes they use after completing each hole of the course. Then they write down the total in the corresponding box on the scorecard.
Although they may look a little different, all scorecards contain common information.

They all have a line called a "Hole" row, which corresponds to each hole of the course. They will also contain rows that indicate which tees are played and the yardages of each hole. The colors used for the individual rows varies according to the course.

The following scorecard also includes the layout of each hole at the top:

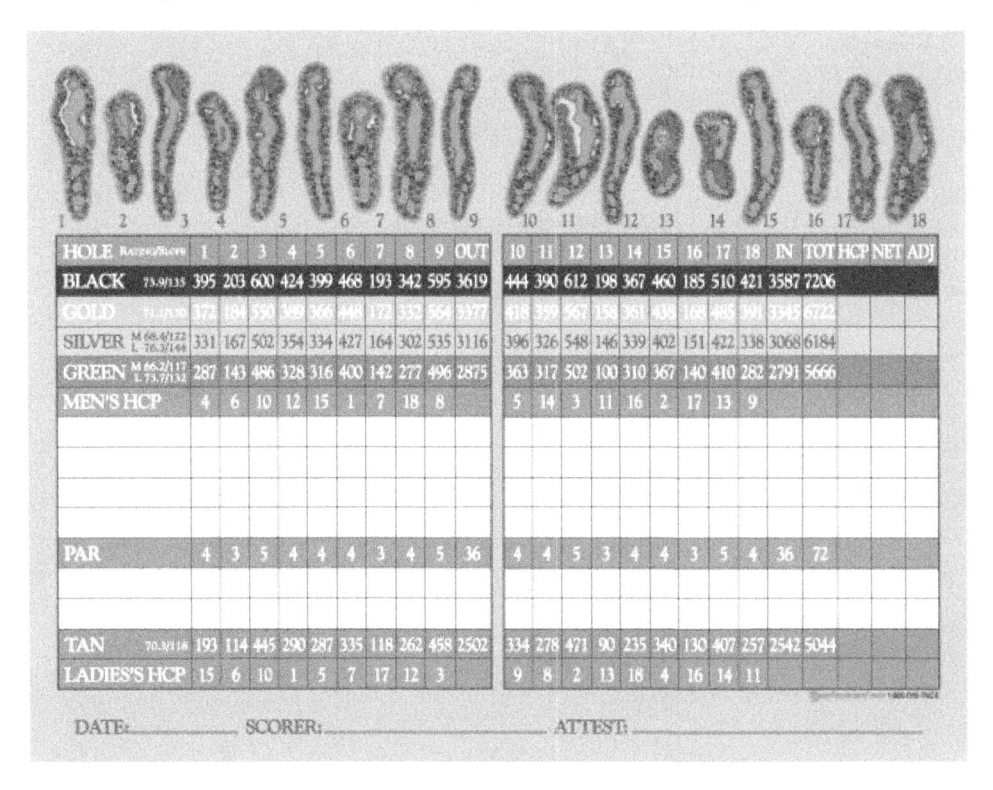

HOLE	Rating/Slope	1	2	3	4	5	6	7	8	9	OUT	10	11	12	13	14	15	16	17	18	IN	TOT	HCP	NET	ADJ
BLACK	75.9/135	395	203	600	424	399	468	193	342	595	3619	444	390	612	198	367	460	185	510	421	3587	7206			
GOLD	73.1/130	372	184	550	389	366	448	172	332	564	3377	418	359	567	158	361	438	168	485	391	3345	6722			
SILVER	M 68.4/122 L 76.3/144	331	167	502	354	334	427	164	302	535	3116	396	326	548	146	339	402	151	422	338	3068	6184			
GREEN	M 66.2/117 L 73.7/132	287	143	486	328	316	400	142	277	496	2875	363	317	502	100	310	367	140	410	282	2791	5666			
MEN'S HCP		4	6	10	12	15	1	7	18	8		5	14	3	11	16	2	17	13	9					
PAR		4	3	5	4	4	4	3	4	5	36	4	4	5	3	4	4	3	5	4	36	72			
TAN	70.3/118	193	114	445	290	287	335	118	262	458	2502	334	278	471	90	235	340	130	407	257	2542	5044			
LADIES'S HCP		15	6	10	1	5	7	17	12	3		9	8	2	13	18	4	16	14	11					

DATE: _____ SCORER: _____ ATTEST: _____

Course Handicaps

You may also notice rows with corresponding numbers showing Men's or Ladies Handicaps. They're used to help beginners even the playing field on the course.

Consult the chart to determine where you can reduce your score by one or more points or "take a stroke". Depending on your course handicap, you may end up taking strokes on several holes.

If you have a handicap of 5, you need to take a stroke form each of the five highest-rated holes on the scorecard. Bear in mind that 1 is considered the highest and 18 is the lowest.

If you are a real beginner, you may end up with a handicap of 18. This means you get to take a point from every hole of the entire course!

You should mark the holes where you use a handicap with a small dot. You should also use a forward slash to divide the corresponding boxes for these holes. Your actual number of strokes gets entered on the top and your net score (your actual score minus your course handicap) gets entered below.

Common Statistics

Players may also choose to record statistics on the scorecard. Some of the more common statistics include:

- **Fairways Hit** – This means your ball reaches the fairway with a tee shot.

- **Putts Taken** – This refers to the number of putts you use for each hole.

- **Greens In Regulation (GIR)** – This indicates whether your ball reaches the putting surface in 1 shot for a Par 3, 2 shots for a Par 4 or 3 shots for a Par 5 hole.

Circles & Squares

You may see scorecards with circles or squares surrounding some of the stroke totals. The circles represent holes that are below par, squares represent above par holes and the remaining numbers equal par holes. Some totals may be surrounded by two circles or squares.

Here is the meaning of the symbols:

> One Circle   = Birdie
> Two Circles   = Eagle
> One Square   = Bogey
> Two Squares   = Double Bogey

We included this information so you'll understand the symbols if you see them.

However, beginners shouldn't worry about this system. There's no point filling up a scorecard with squares until you gain more practice!

How to Use a Ball Washer

Almost every course has a device called a ball washer. In fact, some courses provide one at every single hole! The ball washer was invented in 1934 and as the name implies, it's used to clean your golf balls during a game.

Although each ball washer may look slightly different, they all contain essential parts. They all include a round handle near the top and a long plastic body made containing water. Some ball washers may contain a detergent solution. Inside the body, strong bristles scrub away dirt and debris from your ball. A trash can or towel may be attached to some machines.

Why Use One?

Ball washers are very important because clean balls offer a better shot. A clean ball will travel farther and offer better backspin. It's easier to make clean contact with a clubface when using a clean ball.

Because golf balls have a rough surface, they tend to collect a lot of debris. Dirt, sand or parts of the turf interfere with the special aerodynamics of a golf ball and affect its trajectory.

This debris can transfer to the grooves or face of your club.

Method Used

1. Locate the nearest ball washer on the course

2. Grab the ball on top of the handle and pull straight up

3. You will notice a curved arm containing a hole where you place your ball

4. Move the arm up and down several times. Each time you do this, the bristles inside the machine will clean your ball.

5. Once you're finished, tap one side of the ball until it falls out at the top.

6. If a towel is attached, use it to dry your ball or use your own towel.

You are now ready to return to the course and hit that perfect shot!

How to Repair a Divot

Have you ever taken a big swing and then watched as a piece of turf went flying through the air right after your ball?
This is a very common occurrence in golf. After taking a good swing, you will likely produce what is called a "divot" on the fairway. A divot is defined as "a piece of turn torn up by a golf club in striking a ball". A golf ball can also leave a mark upon contact with the putting surface and is sometimes referred to as a "pitch mark".
Divots are a normal part of golf and are only considered problems if they aren't repaired correctly. Proper golf etiquette requires that you repair any damage that you do to the course during your game.

Why Should You Repair a Divot?

One reason is that leaving a divot will create an uneven playing surface which is unfair for the other players. An important example of this occurred in the final round of the 1998 US Open. Payne Stewart hit a perfect tee shot straight down the fairway. Unfortunately, when he approached his ball, he discovered that it had landed in an unrepaired divot mark!

Another reason to repair divots is because the grass in that specific area may die if the damage isn't fixed quickly enough. In fact, the grass may take 2-3 times longer to grow back in areas of the course that haven't been properly repaired.

Methods Used

Basically, there are 2 methods to repair divots:

1. Fill a divot with sand or a mixture of seed and sand. Make sure to fill the damaged area completely and then pat the sand down with your foot to smooth the area.

2. Find the piece of turf or sod that was removed and try to put it back in place. Hopefully you created a "clean" divot which means the turf was removed in one piece. If not, find as many of the pieces as possible and attempt to replace them as best you can. Then pat the area gently with your foot to smooth the surface.

You may be wondering how to determine which method to use.

The answer is very simple.

If a course wants you to use sand or a sand and seed mixture, they will provide it for you. They will attach a container that looks like a large cup holder to the golf cart. The container is usually attached to the frame of the cart.

If you don't see a container of sand, the course wants you to repair divots by replacing the turf manually.

Using a Divot Repair Tool

You can also use a two-pronged device called a "divot repair tool". When used properly, this tool will help you repair the damage you have caused to a course.

Method

1. Locate the mark left by your ball

2. Insert the divot repair tool into the outer edge of the divot, angled at approximately 45 degrees

3. Gently work the turf up and push it forward back into place

4. Repeat around the entire mark until the area is restored

Note: Don't inset the divot tool directly underneath the area or you'll expose the soil and damage the root system. Also be sure not to insert the tool and twist it or you will break off even more of the turf.

If you have enough time, don't be afraid to repair someone else's divot in addition to your own. You can do your part to ensure a positive experience for the other players.

Your fellow golfers and the course green keepers will appreciate your help.

How to Rake Sand Bunkers

Sand bunkers or sand traps are found on nearly every golf course to make the game more challenging. The picture below shows 2 sand bunkers – one on the lower left and another on the upper right.

All sand traps will contain a device called a rake. This object looks very much like an ordinary garden rake.

Proper golf etiquette requires you to rake the sand with this object if your ball lands in a sand bunker. This process is actually very easy once you learn how to do it properly.

- Locate the lowest spot of the bunker that is close to where your ball landed. This will become your entry and exit point.

Walking down a steep part of the bunker will cause erosion and damage the turf and stepping off a higher edge of the rim will leave deeper footprints by.

You also need to remember that the farther distance you walk, the more area of sand you will need to rake!

- Once you find the lowest point, enter the bunker with your rake. Contrary to popular belief, this action is permitted on any course.

    Just don't use the rake to test the sand conditions or improve your lie. These actions are against the rules and will cost you a penalty stroke.

- After you play your shot, use the rake to sweep the area where your club contacted the sand and your footprints. Pull the rake towards you as you move backwards towards the rim of the bunker.

Make sure not to pull too much sand. Just rake enough so that the surface of the sand is even and no divot marks or footprints are visible.

- Once you have finished raking, exit the bunker and rake the area a few more times.

Where to Leave the Rake

At this point, you may wonder where you should leave the rake.

It's important to place the rake where it has the least chance of affecting another player's ball.

The rules whether you should place the rake outside or inside the bunker depend on the particular course. Most courses will reveal the rules on their scorecard or posted on bulletin boards inside their clubhouse.

If you're in doubt, always leave the rake outside of the bunker.

As noted by the USGA: "There is not a perfect answer for the position of rakes, but on balance it is felt there is less likelihood of an advantage or disadvantage to the player if rakes are placed outside of bunkers."

The main thing is to leave the sand bunkers in the same good condition you found them!

How to Clean Your Golf Clubs

Cleaning Your Irons

It's very important to clean your golf clubs, especially if you play often. Cleaning your clubs will prolong their life and allow you to strike the ball more effectively. Grass, dirt and mud that cling to the clubs can interfere with your shots.

One option is to purchase a special golf club cleaning kit. These kits are usually sold in most pro golf shops.

However, there is a very easy and less expensive method. You will only require the following basic equipment:

- Plastic bucket (if you don't use a sink)

- Mild dishwashing detergent

- Brush with soft plastic bristles (an old toothbrush works great)
- Old towel for drying

Method:

1. Add a little detergent to the bucket
2. Fill with warm water until suds form. Don't use very hot water as it can damage the clubs
3. Take clubs outside if you have access to a hose or place them in a tub or sink
4. Place the irons in the bucket until the heads are completely covered with water
5. Soak clubs for a few minutes. This loosens the dirt in the grooves of the clubface and breaks down the oils and course chemicals on the clubheads
6. Remove each club separately and scrub it with a brush. This cleans any dirt, grass and other debris from the clubface and is the most important step of the entire process.
7. Drag the brush across the sole of the iron and the back of the clubhead
8. To remove any dirt that has hardened over time, soak the irons for a longer period or use a stiffer brush. Never use a brush with wire bristles as it may damage the clubs.
9. Rinse each clubhead off with a hose or tap. Try not to splash water on the shaft of the clubs
10. Take a look to make sure all dirt is removed. If not, repeat the process
11. Use an old towel to dry the clubheads
12. Drag the towel up the shaft of the clubs to remove loose dirt

Note: Never place clubs back in your bag while they are still wet

Cleaning Your Woods

The process for cleaning your woods is a little different from cleaning your irons. You should never submerge any woods made of persimmon or metal woods because this can ruin their finish.

- Quickly dip them into sudsy water or rub them with a moist cloth

- Dry them with a cloth or towel

- Use a brush with soft bristles to clean out the grooves on each wood

How to Clean Your Golf Club Grips

The grip is one of the most important parts of your golf club. Basically, the grip is what connects you to your club. The grip is where your hands make contact with the club and allows you to control all of your shots.

Over time, grime and dirt build up on the grips. The oil from your hands and chemicals from the golf course can add to the problem. Unfortunately, many golfers neglect grips completely. They don't realize that cleaning your grips will prolong their life and give you a better feel when you're taking a shot.

The good news is there are several ways to easily clean the grips. You can go to a pro shop where they can clean your grips for a fee. However, you can complete this task yourself with relatively little effort or expense.

You can wipe them with a moist cloth and then dry them with another cloth. You can also spray on a mild cleanser such as Windex and then wipe it off.

The following method takes a little longer, but is more effective at removing the build up of dirt and grime:

- Fill your sink with warm water and add enough dish detergent to form lots of suds. Don't use really hot water as they may damage the grips.

- Use a wet cloth or a soft bristle brush to grab the suds and rub them into the grip of each club.

- Rinse each grip under running water to remove all of the detergent. Try not to get any water on the shafts during the process.

- As soon as they're rinsed, dry each grip off with a dry cloth or towel. Dry the shaft if they are wet.

You should clean your grips on a regular basis to make them last longer and perform better.

Eventually your grips will need to be replaced. With age and exposure to the elements, the material will crack and your grips will harden and start to come loose.

This will affect your game negatively. More importantly, loose grips can injure another player if they come completely loose or cause you to lose control of your club after a swing. Experts advise that you change your grips every season if you play more than 20 rounds.

50 Golf Tips for Lady Golfers

There is always something new to learn in the strategic game of golf. Even professionals continue to perfect their shots and learn more about the game. However, beginners need to learn the basics before progressing to more advanced shots. We're going to provide you with a wide range of beginner golf tips that will help you improve your game and reduce your frustration level.

Keep these tips in mind, the next time you're on the course or at the driving range. You are sure to improve both your swing and your score!

Tip 1: Putting Games

As a beginner, you probably need to improve your short putts. If so, try putting to a dime. This exercise will improve your focus and concentration. Here is another great putting drill: try sinking five balls in a row starting one foot away, and then increasing to two feet, three feet and so on. Continue until you miss a shot at which point you have to start all over again! Don't increase your distance until you have sunk all 5 balls in a row. You can practice these drills while waiting to tee off.

Tip 2: Pull The Rope!

If you have a slice problem, you most likely cut across the ball during your downswing. You need to learn the correct path for the clubhead. An easy way to accomplish this is to picture a rope attached to an overhead tree. At the top of your backswing, imagine pulling the rope straight down. This will bring your right elbow close to your side and provides your stroke the correct inside path. It will also enable you to swing out towards the target instead of across the ball.

Tip 3: Hold Up the Ball

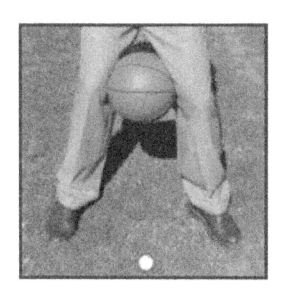

You may be collapsing your left knee toward the right during your backswing. This action forces your shoulders to drop and your hips to sway and overturn. To correct this problem, picture your left knee moving out toward the target during the backswing. You should feel tension and stability in both knees. If this doesn't feel right, try imagining you're holding a basketball between your knees. This should do the trick!

Tip 4: Be a Hitchhiker

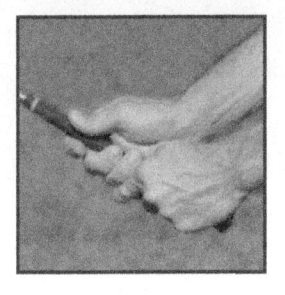

During your backswing, visualize placing your right hand in the hitchhiker position. When the club is at waist height, you should be able to look back and see your thumb pointing to the sky. You can also picture your hand in a handshake position with your palm facing neither up nor down. These visualizations will you correct the beginning of your swing!

Tip 5: Pause at the Top

Many beginners tend to swing too quickly. Although you do need to swing with power and acceleration, you also need to maintain a rhythm. Take a slight pause at the top of your backswing before you change direction and begin your downswing. Try this and you'll discover that your ball will land in the middle of the fairway more often!

Tip 6: Eye on a Dime

Having trouble putting? Try this simple drill. Place the ball on top of a dime and focus your eyes on the dime throughout your stroke. Avoid the temptation to follow the ball with your eyes as soon as you have hit the ball, especially for short putts. Just continue to focus on the dime, rather than following the ball with your eyes, head and shoulders.

Tip 7: See Yourself in the Clubface

You need to keep your clubface "open" if you want to get out of the greenside bunkers. Closing the face results in a lower trajectory and causes your club to dig in the sand. Try this trick: Image that your clubface is a mirror and you will see your reflection in it at the end of your sand shot. This ensures you take your club all the way to eye level and that you keep it open all the way to the finish.

Tip 8: Check Your V's!

Many factors contribute to a slice. The most common is your grip. Here's a method you can use to fix this problem: When you are looking down during your address, make sure you can see the first 2 knuckles of your left hand and a "V" formed between your thumb and forefinger pointing toward your right shoulder. With your right hand, have the "V" pointing toward your chin or slightly to your right shoulder.

Tip 9: Bulls eye!

Three-foot putts can be a problem if you let them. Why not follow the strategy used by Seve Ballesteros, one of the all time great putters. Imagine a bulls eye attached to the back of the cup. This encourages you to accelerate the putter through and keep the clubface moving square to the hole!

Tip 10: Shoulder Under Chin – You Won't Hit It Thin!

Do you have a problem topping the ball or "hitting it thin"? If so, get in the habit of placing your right shoulder under your chin before looking to see where the ball lands. Don't keep your head down forever. You can let your head move, but allow your shoulder to bring it up after contact. If you do this correctly, you'll see the club hit the ball almost every time!

Tip 11: Step on It!

Practice proper weight shift by stepping with your right foot over your left after you hit the ball. You should feel as if you're walking to the right after contact. After each swing, ask yourself where the weight is. On your right or on left foot? A proper, balanced position should be 90% on your left foot and 10% on your right toe. Your momentum will naturally carry you to the walking position with right over left.

Tip 12: Hit Far With the Ball Forward

Depending on the club you're using, your position over the ball will vary. For example, the ball should be in the middle of your stand when using shorter irons such as 7, 8, 9 or PW. As the left of the club decreases, the ball should be incrementally farther towards your front foot until it is just inside your left heel when hitting the woods. If you want to hit a lower shot, remember that the ball should be back in the stance. The ball should be forward for higher shots.

Tip 13: Rock-Solid Right Knee

During your backswing, you have to keep your weight on the inside of your right foot and maintain a slight bend in your knee. If you don't, you end up with poor contact and a loss of power. As you take your club back, imagine that your right knee is braced and solid as a wall. This will help your upper body coil behind the ball so you can make an aggressive move through it and send it soaring!

Tip 14: Grip It Light On the Right

Normally your right side needs to remain solid for a strong shot, but not your grip. Many golfers grip their club too tightly with their right hand which leads to extra tension. This can also make you swing "over the top" and cut across the ball. Try this fix: Check your right side grip, arm and shoulder tension before you swing. You should sense a muscle tension corresponding to a 6-7 on a scale of 1 to 10. Light muscles are always better than tight muscles!

Tip 15: Muscle It!

Remember that golf isn't just a wrist game. You need to use the big muscles in your legs and trunk to achieve a powerful swing. Many beginners tend to hit the ball using only their arms and wrists. You may connect once in a while using this method. However, you need use your entire body, not just part of it for real consistency and power. Learn to muscle it!

Tip 16: Go Cross Hand

A very common putting error involves a breakdown of the wrists. Try using a cross hand grip. Place your left hand down the grip where you right hand would normally be and then place your right hand on top of the grip. This may feel strange at first, but it will force your hands to work together as one unit. This is one of the fundamentals of good putting. Remember to always keep your hands in front of the ball and your left wrist flat during your stroke!

Tip 17: Splash Some Sand

The next time you find yourself in a bunker, focus on sliding a thin "divot" of sand from under the ball and on to the green. Open your clubface a few degrees clockwise and line up slightly to your left. Then splash the sand towards your target and your ball will follow!

Tip 18: Putt with Your Eyes Closed!

Have you ever tried to play golf with your eyes closed? You may be surprised at the answer. If you practice putting with your eyes shut, you will find it easier to feel your body movements. You should feel your shoulders working like a pendulum. The next thing you know, you will hear the ball hitting the bottom of that cup!

Tip 19: Hit Low Into the Wind

Many players tend to hit harder into a breeze. This actually causes them to put more spin on the ball and hit it higher. To hit a lower, more controlled shot, put the ball back in your stance a few inches and keep your hands forward. Use a longer club than normal and swing easy. If you have trouble, remember this saying "Swing with ease into the breeze".

Tip 20: Wiggle Your Toes

Many golfers tend to move farther from the ball at address over time. Make sure you don't reach for the ball or place too much weight on the balls of your feet. Here is a test you can try: wiggle your toes at address. This may sound funny, but it will ensure that you don't place too much weight on the forward part of your foot!

Tip 21: Don't Choke It To Death!

Beginning golfers may assume they have to grip the club hard to hit hard. Actually, the opposite is true. A tense muscle is a slow muscle. Clubhead speed is essential for distance and light muscles always work faster. Try to attain a grip pressure of 5-6 on a scale of 1 to 10. Remember to grip your club lightly to hit the ball far!

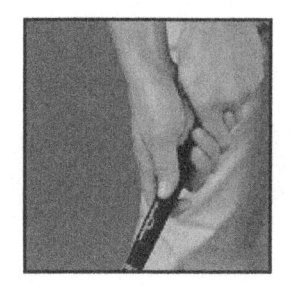

Tip 22: Weight Distribution Is Vital When Chipping

Proper weight distribution is essential to consistently getting the ball up and down. At least 60% of your weight should remain on your front foot at address or your left foot if you are a right-handed golfer. Picture hitting slightly down and through the ball. This encourages a proper transfer of weight and will help you complete the follow-through. Keep the back of your left wrist facing the target. If you let your wrist break down, your shows will break down as well!

Tip 23: Use Club Loft to Your Advantage

Make sure to hit down and through the ball if you want to send it airborne. If you let your club's loft to do the work, you'll achieve good contact and a natural flight path. Golf clubs have loft for a reason so always use it to your advantage!

Tip 24: Keep Your Head Still

Keeping your head still is essential for solid contact and consistent putting. Focus on not moving your head well after impact. Head movement causes your shoulders to open and your putter to cut across the ball. You can also try putting with your eyes closed. You may be surprised at the positive results!

Tip 25: The Toe Is Your Best Friend

Downhill putts are often fast and difficult. Therefore, why not take a tip from the experts: Hit the ball on the toe of your putter, not on the sweet spot. This reduces the jump on the ball and prevents it from traveling past the hole. Remember, not to do this on uphill putts!

Tip 26: Bowl Your Way to Better Putting

You may be experiencing difficulty with putting distance control. If so, try standing in golf like address position and rehearsing several strokes without your putter. Then take a ball in your hand and roll the ball toward the hole. Once you feel comfortable determining how hard to roll the ball, pick up your putter and use the same motion to hit the ball!

Tip 27: Putt to the Pro Side of the Cup

Watch a pro when they are lining up a breaking putt. You'll notice how they always favor the "high" side of the hole, rather than the "low" side. The law of averages indicates that that gravity will work in your favor if the ball is above the hole as your putt is breaking near it. If your ball is breaking away on the low side, gravity will work against you. Just remember the pro side, not the low side and you'll sink more putts!

Tip 28: Swing Easy when it's Breezy

When you're playing in the wind, remember this simple, but effective saying "swing with ease into the breeze". This will prevent you from over swinging in the wind and your ball from sailing too high. Greg Norman used this tip during his 1994 British Open win!

Tip 29: Solidify Your Swing's Foundation

A smooth tempo and proper balance is necessary for a consistent golf swing. Just as a house requires a solid foundation, so does your golf swing does. Practice hitting several shots with your feet approximately 6 inches apart. This improves your balance, tempo and rhythm and is very effective when you return to your normal stance when hitting.

Tip 30: Turn Your Way to More Distance

When hitting a golf ball a long distance, you need to minimize your hip turn and maximize your shoulder turn. The easiest way is to keep your right knee firm and flexed throughout, and ensure that your left knee doesn't slide to the right during your backswing. Use the opposite knee if you are left-handed. You also need to get your shoulder behind the ball at the top of your backswing. This will ensure a proper weight shift and permit a longer swing.

Tip 31: Release Is the Key to Distance

The key to improving distance is a proper hand release during your swing. Take a short backswing and stop as soon as your club and hands are at waist level. Look as if you're shaking hands with your thumb pointing to the sky. As you swing down into the follow-through, ensure your hands are in the same position as your backswing (thumb facing up). This technique forces you to use your hands properly.

Tip 32: Swing through the Ball, Not At It

Most consistent, powerful swings have one thing in common – extension through the ball after hitting it. You can perfect this b placing a tee approximately 8 inches in front of the ball you're hitting. Try to hit not only the ball, but also the tee. This will train you to swing through the ball, rather than at it.

Tip 33: Make a Smooth Transition

Many amateur golfers ruin their opportunity to make solid contact by starting their downswing with a tense, violent motion. The top of the swing is a critical transition point and should lead quietly into a smooth downswing. An effective strategy is to think "light and lazy" at the top of your swing.

Tip 34: Remember, It's Just a Game

It's very important to remember that everyone plays golf to have fun. Too often, players become overly anxious about their performance. You can still try hard and concentrate on your swing. Just don't let the pursuit of perfection ruin your enjoyment of the game. Performance anxiety can interfere with the freedom of your swing and your spirit. Golf is just a game. Adopt this attitude at your very first tee and your performance and comfort level will rise!

Tip 35: Avoid Over Analysis Paralysis

These tips won't help if you become overly tense or analytical. Having a strong desire to improve is great, but you have to learn to relax. After a practice session or a game, hit a percentage of your shots with only the target in mind. This involves watching where you want the ball to travel, thinking positively and letting it go. Just grip the club and swing away!

Tip 36: Take It Back Low & Slow

Amateurs often take the club back too quickly with their wrists. This reduces proper tension and causes their swing to go off plane. Here's an effective drill to help you gain the proper feel for the take-away. Get into your normal address position and then place a ball behind your clubhead. As you start your backswing, roll the ball backward. Continue rolling the ball until it's well past your right foot. You'll feel your opposite shoulder move beneath your chin. You'll realize how straight your left arm should be during your backswing.

Tip 37: Pass the Pole for More Distance

You need to use a proper weight shift to achieve maximum distance and consistency. Imagine a pole arising vertically from the ground where the ball is resting during address. During your take-away, concentrate on getting your left shoulder behind the ball and the imaginary pole without swaying your hips. This ensures a proper position to initiate your downswing. During your follow-through, move your right shoulder past the ball and imaginary pole. When performed correctly, you will make a good turn and proper weight shift.

Tip 38: Improve Your Balance & Game

If find it difficult to make good contact, you're most likely starting to sway, losing your balance or not turning. The following drill will help: Start by using short swings to hit shots with your feet approximately 6 inches apart. This exercise promotes proper footwork, balance and a free swing with your arms. It will also force you to turn more - you'll fall over if you don't! Once you feel comfortable making good contact, you can increase the length of your swings.

Tip 39: Make a Steep Swing in the Sand

This exercise will help you learn to take the club back in a more upright plane out of a bunker. By taking your club back more abruptly, you increase your changes of getting under the ball properly and impacting the sand more precisely. Have someone stand behind you in the sand and hold a rake approximately 2 feet behind your ball at a 45° angle. The goal is to swing up the rake handle as if your plane is steeper than your normal swing. Take several swings using this method and you'll find yourself hitting high, soft shots from the bunker!

Tip 40: Remember the Practice Area

The first place a pro golfer visits before heading to the first tee in a tournament is the practice area. You should also get in the habit of following this routine. Remember, you can warm up and loosen your muscles there, rather than worrying about how you're striking the ball. Once you're ready to hit, start with a wedge and then work your way down the set until you reach the driver. Finish with a few wedges. This promotes a proper tempo and feel which are vital to striking the ball correctly and can also prevent injuries!

Tip 41: Learn To Stay Flexible

Loss of flexibility and a resulting poor turn (like the one in the photo) is a very common complaint. The hip blocker is a very effective drill. When you fix your knees, your upper body is forced to turn more correctly and slowly increase flexibility. As you swing, remember to turn your shoulders as far back as possible until your left shoulder is under your chin. You will feel a greater stretch along your left side. Finish by repeating this on your follow-through, but with your right shoulder under your chin. You'll eventually increase your ability to coil fully without using your hips. Remember, the power in your swing comes from a big shoulder turn and a minimal hip turn.

Tip 42: Increase Your Forearm Strength

Golf success requires left wrist and forearm strength. Many golfers break down their left wrist with their right arm dominating through impact. This causes many problems such as topping, loss of distance and shots pulling to the left. An effective strengthening drill involves holding the club straight out in front of you using the last 3 fingers of your left hand. Use your wrists to move the club up and down 10-12 times. Three slow, controlled sets without bending your arm will set the proper motion into your muscle memory.

Tip 43: Start at the Top

The secret to hitting a straighter, more consistent shot is to maintain a square clubface at impact. If your clubface connects squarely with the ball, your shots will fly straight. One way to promote this is by maintaining a square clubface at the top of your backswing. If your club isn't square, you need to manipulate it on impact which causes many timing problems. This drill is effective for teaching you how to play from a square position. With a club in your hand, lift your arms up to your forehead and rotate your shoulders as far as possible, allowing a full backswing. This places your hands in a square position at the top and encourages a complete turn. Try to hold this position for a few seconds so you get the proper feeling at the top of the swing.

Tip 44: Act like a Baseball Player

A controlled, but aggressive weight shift is required for a proper golf swing. However, many players get stuck on their right foot and don't completely shift which causes poor shots. Try teeing a ball and adopting your normal address position. Then bring your left foot back so your feet are approximately 6 inches apart. Take a normal backswing, but just as begin down, step forward as if you were a home run hitter stepping on to the pitch. You may need to down your swing to hit the ball solidly. This will give you an accurate feeling of shifting and train you repeat the motion.

Tip 45: Stabilize Your Left Knee

Longer hitters display a significant inconsistency between hip and shoulder turn. A big hip turn is required during your follow-through, not your backswing! Your left knee is an important body part that affects what your hips do. When it collapses or bends inward, your hips turn too much which makes it impossible to create the necessary torque to build clubhead speed. An easy solution is to feel your left knee remaining outward toward the target at the top of your backswing. This maintains distance between your knees.

Tip 46: Turn & Burn

There's an easy way to give you the feeling of a proper shoulder turn without your hips getting too involved. Sit on the edge of a golf cart and put a club on the line of your shoulders to simulate address. Then turn back and try to get the shaft pointing straight in front of you. You'll feel a lot of stretch on your left side which is good. This will help you get behind the ball more efficiently and will result in a few extra yards.

Tip 47: Dirty Those Shoes

You can tell a lot about golfers by looking at their shoes. If their shoes are older and their right toe is completely clean, there's a problem. When you shift your weight properly, you end up balanced on your right toe. This action eventually wears down that toe. Try to get your right toe dirty and beat up! This indicates that you are shifting your weight properly.

Tip 48: Point Your Way to Consistency

The direct action of your hands affects the position of your clubface and the flight of your ball. Take your grip and adopt a normal stance, but point your finger down the shaft so it's pointing at the ball at address. Check the club when it's parallel to the ground on both your backswing and follow-through. Your finger should point down the target line on the return and at the target on the way.

Tip 49: Use Both Sides

For many players, your right side dominates a weak left arm and side during downswing and through impact. This causes poor extension and other swing flaws. Swing lightly with your left arm only to maintain a proper feel. As you do this, check how your arm extends freely through the impact zone. Then add your right arm with a light grip and try to maintain the previous extended feeling. You'll feel it becoming more restricted right away. Just let it go and continue to use your left arm and side along with your right. You have two sides so you might as well use them both!

Tip 50: Swing inside the Barrel

Golfers often continue to widen their stance. This is good for stability, but it permits lateral movement which can develop into a sway. The barrel drill can correct this. Keeping your stance approximately shoulder width apart, imagine 2 straight lines coming out of the ground outside your heels. This allows for some lateral movement, but a full turn is normally required to avoid hitting the lines. Visualize yourself swinging in the barrel and wait for the low scores to follow!

Golf Lessons

Now that you've had a chance to review our 50 Golf Tips, we're going to provide you with 25 Lessons. These will help you improve your scores and deal with a wide variety of common techniques and problems.

These lessons are great for beginners and more advanced Lady Golfers alike.

Lesson 1: Six Habits That Will Help Your Handicap

The simplest advice often pays the greatest dividends. That's been our experience for many years. Most golfers hope for a magic tip or want to be enlightened about the intricacies of grip, stance and posture. However, all they really need are some good golf habits!

So here is our list of the six top ways to lower your scores and your handicap:

1. Move Up

Having trouble achieving a mental breakthrough? Try playing from the forward tees to alter your comfort zone and lower your scores. Playing a shorter course will instill a "go-for-par" or birdie mindset that will stick with you when you return to your accustomed tees. If you can't score any better from the forward tees, consider it a message that you require extra work on your short game!

2. Do It Daily

Ben Hogan once said he hated to miss a day of practice because it meant one more day before he could get better. While you may not be able to keep this regimen, you should keep in mind that you get out what you put into the game. Pressed for time? Just taking a club out in the backyard and swinging for 15 minutes will help.

3. When You Play Golf, Play Golf

If you're going to take the time to play, do it seriously and focus on each shot. Never make a careless swing during a serious round! Of course, this doesn't mean you can't have fun. It just means you should turn up the focus. Use the driving range for working on technical skills and the golf course for focusing on the real target: lowering your score!

4. Purchase Better Gear

We're not saying you should spend thousands of dollars on equipment. But if you're using an older set that isn't fitted properly, you may be holding yourself back. Many recent technical advances such as perimeter weighting to produce a larger sweet spot and larger club head volumes will make a difference in the consistency and distance of your shots. Why not take advantage of them?

5. Don't Shortchange Your Short Game

Chipping and putting account for more than half the strokes in a typical golfer's game. Consequently, you should devote most of your practice to your short game. I like to use a football analogy: It's great to be able to advance to the two-yard line, but it won't mean a thing if you can't make it into the end zone!

6. Write It Down!

It's easier to improve if you can document your hits and misses. Where do you hit good shots, and where do you hit poor ones? Did you hit right, left, or on top? How many putts of less than five feet do you miss? Keep a journal and consult it periodically to unearth patterns and discover areas that need work.

Good luck and have fun!

Lesson 2: How to Develop the Perfect Pre-Shot Routine

Most skilled golfers have a pre-shot routine – rituals that include everything from the way they approach the ball to how they waggle.

These routines serve a good purpose. When you approach your shots the same way each time, you train your subconscious to be less affected by outside influences such as pressure, wind, spectators or jibes from your foursome. Fewer variables in the moments leading up to your swing will mean fewer variables during your swing.

How should you develop your personal pre-shot routine? Here are some guidelines:

1. Do What Works For You

Factors such as how you arrive at your grip and stance, look at the target, waggle the club and take practice swings are all personal preferences. The exact details are less important than performing the same action consistently. Many pros even time themselves from start to finish to get within seconds on each swing – you might want to do the same. A good routine won't take a lot of time. Quickly, but methodically, review the checklist, think positive and hit the ball. Your ritual should give you a positive feeling about the shot. Once you've completed the routine, trust it, be target oriented and let it go. You don't want to start wondering about your grip or the depth of the water during your backswing!

2. Get Lined Up

Try this in practice: Lay a club on the ground next to the ball and aim it toward the target. Then take a look at the club from behind to ensure it's positioned correctly. Put another club parallel to it close to where your feet would be. For your shot to go straight, the "foot line" should face slightly left of the target. You should also ensure that your knees, hips and shoulders are aligned. Practice this a few times and then perform it without clubs on the ground. Alignment is one of the simplest mistakes to correct. Poor alignment is one of the most destructive, because you must compensate for it in your swing.

3. See It Happen

Skilled players talk about "feeling" a good shot before it occurs. You can develop this feeling by creating a positive image of the ball's flight before you hit it. This visualization prevents negative thoughts. Stand behind the ball and imagine it traveling straight toward the target before landing softly on the green. Or picture a great shot from the past just like the one you're about to make. For beginners, a realistic goal might be to "see" the ball getting up in the air. Studies have shown that players tend to achieve the result they envision. The mind has enormous control over the body so use it to see what you want, not what you don't want! Be target-oriented rather than trouble-oriented.

4. Reflect On Your Successes

When you hit a good shot, soak it in! Watch the ball's flight and how it lands and rolls. Hold your finish and try to mentally reinforce what the swing felt like. Giving yourself this positive feedback will make it much easier to recall these images and feelings during your pre-shot routine. When poor shots occur (as they do for all of us), don't spend too much time thinking about them. Devote your mental energy to producing good shots!

Lesson 3: Five Steps to Develop the Perfect Putt

Putting is often called a game within a game because many of the skills you require to be a good putter differ from those required for the rest of the game. In fact, studies show that putting accounts for 43% of the shots among better players. You'd be hard-pressed to find a great golfer who isn't a skilled putter!

Given these facts, it makes sense for time-pressed golfers to focus on their putting. Ironically, most students ask for tips on everything but putting. If you're serious about lowering your scores, try following these five simple steps to putting perfection.

1. Position

Position yourself so your eyes are over the intended line of the putt (ball line). Hold your putter loosely and directly under your eyes as you address the putt and let gravity take it straight down. When you look down at your putter, make sure it covers the ball. If not, move forward or backward. Ball position should be slightly forward, toward the left foot. Hands should also be forward. Align the putter shaft with your left forearm. This position promotes a good roll as the ball leaves the putter face.

2. Grip

Your hands should work together as a unit, not spread apart. The farther apart your hands, the more likely you'll use your wrist which isn't desired. The putting stroke originates in the shoulders and arms. Use a normal grip, with 3 fingers of each hand on the club and the others just along for the ride. Use relatively light (5 on a scale of 1-10) grip pressure in order to promote feel.

3. Aim

Find a target and imagine a straight line through the center of your putter. Don't worry about the line your feet make, but ensure the putter face is square to the target. This is the line your stroke should follow. Don't tilt your head or you'll distort the perspective.

4. Stroke

Your putting stroke should be dominated by the shoulders and arms and involve as little wrist movement as possible. Minimize body movement and try not to shift weight or turn the hips. In other words, forget much of what you've learned about the body's role in a full swing!

5. Acceleration

Successful putters have a backswing and follow-through of equal length. This promotes acceleration and aids distance control. One of the most common faults involves players taking the club way back and then stopping at the ball on the down stroke, anticipating the hit. Remember to stroke through the ball, not at it!

Lesson 4: Mastering the Second Most Important Club in Your Bag

It's been said that the driver is the second most important club in your bag, next to your putter. A good drive sets the tone for the rest of the hole. Will you be scrambling just to get back on the fairway, hoping for pars and bogeys, or will you be aggressively aiming for the green and for birdies? By squeezing a few extra yards out of those drives, the subsequent iron shot will be that much easier, as will your chips, putts, and so on:

1. Body Coil

Tiger Woods, Fred Couples and other greats generate tremendous power by coiling the upper body with a big shoulder turn. The hips, however, don't turn nearly as much. This creates tension and torque, not unlike a rubber band being stretched before it's released. How do you accomplish this? Try to keep the right leg and knee solid as you take the club away and fully rotate your shoulders. On the downswing, unwind and rotate through the ball with your hips. Make sure your navel is facing the target at the end of the swing to ensure a full turn.

2. Developing a "Lag"

Successful drivers all have a "lag" in their swing. On the downswing, the wrists must release their energy at some point. *When* this happens is the key. The closer to impact with the ball, the more stored power. Many golfers deliver this source of power near the top of the swing or early on the way down and end up swinging with just arms at contact. This is commonly called "casting"--the opposite of lag. One drill is to cock your wrists at the top of the backswing so that there's a right angle between your arm and club. Pull the club down in slow motion, while doing your best to retain this angle. Try to incorporate this into your full swings and remember to release those wrists through the ball!

3. Swinging With the Entire Body

Some of the biggest muscles in your body are the upper legs and trunk, and you should use them to put power in your swing. On the downswing, your legs should begin the drive and the trunk begins the turn. The bigger muscles have much less chance to twitch under pressure than smaller ones. This is why good swingers seem to move effortlessly–the small muscles are being led by the larger ones. We call this "swinging with the whole body." Try it!

4. Left Arm Straight At the Top

Make sure your left arm is kept relatively straight on the backswing to ensure a wide swing arc. Keep some distance between the hands at the top of the swing and your shoulders and head. This produces more club head speed without swinging any harder. Davis Love III and Vijay Singh are great examples of this. Watch them and internalize what you see!

Lesson 5: Four Tips for Playing Golf in a Gale

When the wind blows, some players' games get blown away with it. Don't let this happen to you. Practice the techniques and what the very best golfers do: Use these adverse conditions to your advantage and learn to love the wind!

1. Playing In a Crosswind

Crosswinds are the most difficult playing situation. These winds will magnify any spin on the ball, and greatly reduce distance. If you slice or hook the ball, a crosswind will magnify the effect. Therefore, it's important to use these winds to your advantage. If you want the ball to land softly, such as on a green, try to curve the shot into the crosswind. If you want more distance, or to have the ball roll when it lands, "ride" the wind by curving it in the same direction as the crosswind. In general: play the ball low.

96

2. The Knockdown Shot

The "knockdown" shot can be used in many situations, but is especially useful in the wind. The key points are to avoid swinging at full speed, and to keep your hands in front of the ball. This hand position should remain at address and through impact. Many knockdown shots finish with the forward swing low and only half completed, with the wrists not fully released and definitely not cupped as in a normal shot. The main goal is to keep the ball low and under control.

3. Playing In a Headwind

This is where the knockdown shot really comes in handy. Play the ball back in the stance toward the right foot. Select more club to decrease trajectory. It's important not to swing as hard as on a regular swing (about 80% of normal). Remember what Greg Norman said on his way to winning the 1996 British Open: "Swing with ease into the breeze." This helps in 2 ways: It keeps the ball from having as much spin, and it won't fly as high, where it's especially susceptible to wind.

4. Playing In a Tailwind

Playing with a tailwind is great for your ego. Use less club and count on the ball flying and rolling longer. The wind also makes your shots travel straighter, even when mishit. If distance and carry are the goal, play the ball forward in the stance and hit it higher. Playing the ball back in the stance, as in the other wind situations, will make it a little easier to control—but remember to plan for the longer roll.

The most important thing in any windy situation is to hit the ball solidly. A well-struck ball will be much less affected than a mishit shot with sidespin. Spins in the wind get exaggerated, so watch out!!

Lesson 6: Finding the Fairway

How often have you birdied or even been able to par a hole after finding trouble off the tee? Hitting the fairway consistently is vital to playing well. However, it's not an easy task, especially in a pressure situation such as a tournament. The following are a few ideas to help you drive your ball in the fairway more often:

1. Visualize the Shot

Creating a **positive visual image** is critical in any sport but it's even more important in golf—a very mental game. The next time you're in the tee box, stand behind the ball and pick a target. Be very specific about your target rather than just aiming out there somewhere. As you stand behind the ball, picture yourself addressing the ball with the proper posture and alignment. Now, focus on the desired ball flight. Picture the ball launching off the clubface—high in the air and heading right toward the target. Think back to a positive drive from another day in the same situation. Finally, step into the address position and let it happen. Remember, "seeing" what you want gives you a much greater ratio of success.

2. Swing within Yourself

Many good drivers will tell you they have a "bread and butter" shot and an all-out shot. When the fairway is wide and the situation allows, it's fine to grip it and rip it. But when you really need to land in the fairway, rely on a swing you can trust. Use the swing that gives you the highest degree of accuracy. This swing is usually an 80% swing speed accompanied by good rhythm and tempo. In addition, reducing the hip turn on the backswing is helpful. Remember, the key to this type of shot is to get the ball on line and rolling. Tiger Woods often used this tee shot during the U.S. and British Opens this year. When executed correctly, your ball will fly low, straight and roll a lot—down the fairway.

3. Stay Balanced

As we mentioned in other lessons, balance is critical in achieving consistent results with the driver and all other parts of the game. After you've swung, you should be able to stand tall with your body fully turned toward the target for a few seconds without losing your footing. If you're at all shaky, it's time for some practice. A good drill is to make a slow and complete practice swing. This slower motion will help to train your muscles. It also makes it easier to keep your balance. Eventually, you'll be able to increase your practice swing speed while retaining the balance at the end of the follow-through.

4. Use the Right Tools

This is the hard part and can take a while if you're just randomly trying clubs. This is where club fitting can really speed up the process of improving your game. No two golf swings are alike. The best club for you might be the worst for someone else. Having the perfect fit is very important in helping you find the fairway.

Lesson 7: Many Players are Afraid of the Right Side. Don't Be!

Students often tell me that they have "too much right-side emphasis" in their swings. They have usually been told this by well-meaning teachers.

In most instances, the right side is getting a bad rap. In reality, it's a golfer's biggest asset! Among right-handed players, it provides most of the power.

You really can't have too much right side in your swing, but you can use it improperly. To illustrate the power your right side possesses, try pushing as hard as you can against a fixed object such as a golf cart that is approximately 3 feet off the ground. Make sure your right elbow is close to your side in front of your right hip. Now try the same thing with your left arm pushing into the cart with the back of your wrist, as in a golf swing. No power there! The reason? The right hand is taking advantage of the full body: trunk, legs and torso. In contrast, the left arm is pulling away from the body, making it difficult to generate power. Like a boxer throwing a punch, you're using a full body rotation with your right side—not just the arm.

1. Drop at the Top

That gets golfers into trouble with the right side is often called "coming over the top." This means that the downswing is being initiated by the upper body, particularly the right shoulder and arm. To correct this, think of your hands and arms lightly dropping for a few inches from the top of the backswing. This puts the right elbow where it should be--close and connected to the right hip as you start to turn *see photo*. Don't try to keep the elbow close on the backswing, however, as this will create a very flat and narrow swing.

2. Get Your Train on Track

The other problem is when the right hand becomes overactive and dominates the left. This causes a breakdown of the left arm and a "cupping" of the wrists. Here's how to fix the problem: Think of the right as the locomotive, and the left as the train tracks. The left channels power down the proper path toward the target. To get a feel for this, swing with the left arm only. As you come through, ensure that the left shoulder turns naturally, and away from the chin. If this doesn't happen, you'll likely see lot s of shots go to the right.

Lesson 8: How to Turn Bunker Play into a Day at the Beach

Let's face it, everyone has to dig themselves out of the sand sooner or later. Fortunately, there are simple, reliable techniques for blasting out of bunkers. Good sand play doesn't just involve technique - equipment is also crucial. Therefore, we have also covered the essential aspects of a good sand wedge.

Read on for everything you need to know so you enjoy your next day at the beach:

My Favorite Tips

- Use swing speed to alter distance. Practice until you can gauge distance by your personal swing speeds.

- Make the clubface enter behind the ball at a steep angle to hit shorter, and a shallower angle to hit longer. A steeper angle allows the club head to get under the ball and lift it.

- Take 2-3 inches of sand with each shot (see photo above). Less sand will spin the ball more, but is risky. Practice by drawing a line in the sand behind the ball and hit that spot.

- Establish firm footing by digging the feet in slightly.

- Use an open stance (left foot spread to the left) to restrict backswing length and steepen the swing.

- Open the clubface slightly to offset the open stance. Open it more if you want a higher, softer shot.

- Keep your wrists firm through impact and don't release your hands until well after impact.

- Visualize a steep, "U-shaped" swing.

Beach Clubs

It's important to understand sand wedge design and how it can work for you. A **well-designed wedge** has three important characteristics:

- "Bounce" describes the rounded sole of the club head. Sand wedges have this to allow the club to glide, skid or bounce rather than dig into the sand.

- "Loft" or angle of the clubface is crucial for getting the ball in the air, over the edges of bunkers, and to ensure that it lands softly. Sand wedges generally have a loft of 56-60 degrees. By comparison, a pitching wedge is 48-52 degrees.

- "Toe-heel camber" is what gives sand wedges an oval-shaped look on the bottom of the face, to prevent the toe or heel from catching. Think of the club "splashing" through the sand rather than digging.

Remember, you're making things unnecessarily difficult if you're using a **pitching wedge** to get out of the sand!

Make It Happen In the Mind's Eye

Tension can ruin your sand shot faster than anything else. When tension occurs, the swing is inhibited and so is the chance for a good shot. Try to visualize a good shot. Stay muscularly light and mentally positive. Gary Player, one of the worlds' best bunker players, once remarked, "If I am one of the greats, it's for one simple reason: no bunker shot has ever scared me and none ever will. Approach every bunker shot with the feeling you are going to hole it."

Lesson 9: Our 6 Best Tips for Hitting From the Rough & Other Tough Lies

I don't care how good a golfer you are--at some point you'll be stuck in a bad lie. It happens to all of us! Getting the ball out of the rough can be quite a challenge--especially if you don't have a strategy. Here are some tips to help bail you out of a bad situation, and just maybe have some fun doing it!

1. Stand Closer At Address

Standing slightly closer to the ball will create a more upright swing plane, which means the club will encounter less grass on the downswing.

2. Open the Clubface

Opening the clubface clockwise at address helps in 2 ways: First, it gives the shot more loft which helps it get airborne. Second, the rough often grabs the clubface and pulls it left, so opening it helps keep the shot on line.

3. Move Your Stance Forward

When using the short irons, moving forward over the ball will promote a steeper swing and help "punch" the ball out without catching too much grass.

4. Adjust Your Distance

Rough tends to take backspin off the ball and create a "flier" that goes farther and takes longer to stop. Adjust your target to allow for the added roll.

5. Use a Steeper Approach

On the downswing, you should feel as though you are hitting "down and through" with a sharper swing. Don't be afraid to move some grass and take a divot. This is one time to be aggressive!

6. Adjust Your Grip

We normally recommend light grip pressure. However, when hitting in the rough, the left hand should be slightly tighter. By doing so, the club won't turn over when it hits the grass or pull the shot to the left..

Lesson 10: Our Best Tips for Hitting out Of a Side Hill Lie

In an ideal world, we wouldn't hit balls into embarrassing lies in the first place. But the fact is, we all do it, no matter how good or well-practiced a golfer we are. Consequently, it pays to know how to get out of these situations!

One of the most difficult is the side hill lie where the ball is above or below your feet.

Here are some tips that will improve your chances of a successful escape:

Ball above the Feet

In this situation, the most common mistake is hitting behind the ball and making it go too far left. To fix these problems you should:

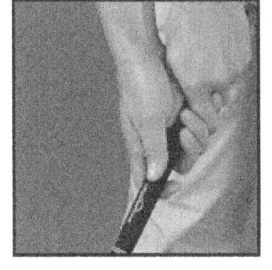

1. Choke down on the club. The amount depends on the severity of the slope.

2. Aim to the right and open the clubface slightly (turn it clockwise). The ball tends to go left from this type of lie because the slope pulls it that way.

3. Reduce knee flex. It's less likely that you will hit the ball "fat" or behind this way.

Ball below the Feet

In this situation, the most common mistake is hitting the ball too far right and topping it. To fix these problems, you should:

1. Grip near the end of the shaft to help avoid hitting it "thin" or on top.

2. Aim slightly left. The ball tends to go right from this type of lie.

3. Use more knee flex. This helps avoid hitting the ball "thin" or on top.

Lesson 11: How to Be At Your Best in the Rain & the Cold

A strong mental attitude is critical when nature's forces are trying to knock you off your game. Try putting these countermeasures in place and you may just learn to love winter!

Rain

Keeping clubs and grips dry is critical when it starts to rain. Once grips get wet, your performance and desire will decrease dramatically. Professionals have caddies to take care of this. The rest of us need to take the time to place a cover or towel over the opening of the bag. If you have an umbrella, hang a couple of dry towels on the spokes. This way you'll always be able to dry off the grips and your hands, no matter how wet every thing else gets. If you wear a glove, remove it after each shot and keep it in a dry place—under the umbrella is a good spot. Invest in some high-quality rain gear. Many of the new, high-tech fabrics really work, keeping you dry without causing you to sweat or get soaked from the inside out.

Also, remember that the ball won't travel as far in the rain, and the ground will be wet, decreasing roll. Many players fail to use enough club in wet conditions.

Cold

When the air is cold, the ball won't travel as far, so you should choose more club here as well. Good chipping and putting can make up for other mistakes in cold conditions, but you must have good feel; this means keeping your hands warm. When US pros play in icy weather at the Dunhill cup in Scotland, they're wear warm gloves between shots and place hand warmers in their pockets. Make sure you have a way to keep your hands warm before you tee off!

You should also choose a softer compression golf ball. This will help you keep a sense of feel around the greens and elsewhere.

Wind is also a major factor in winter. For tips on how to hit when it starts to blow, see our previous lesson on the topic. Remember to have fun out there!

Lesson 12: Our Five Best Tips to Help You Hit Woods with Confidence

You will be probably be playing a fairway wood on the second shot of a long par-5 hole. Woods can always out-distance irons because of their longer shaft length and bigger head. However, they're harder to use.

Because of their length, you can't approach a fairway wood the same way as an iron. Your swing plane needs to be shallower or more horizontal. You want to sweep the grass instead of making a divot.

Practice sweeping the grass until you can consistently hit the target. Then try to hit your target and sweep more grass. You should be able to sweep about 4 inches of grass. You should see blades of grass being flattened and a path being formed. As with all other swings, your hands and arms should be relaxed.

Now that you can consistently sweep the grass, you should be able to sweep the grass when there is a ball lying there. Hopefully, your mind won't be overloaded with the extra image. If you can disregard the presence of the ball and repeat your sweeping swing, you're on your way to mastering the fairway woods.

Like they say, "The ball just happens to be in the way."

Here are a few thoughts to take with you to the range:

1. Make a Full Turn

As your body ages, flexibility diminishes. Don't feel bad, it happens to everyone. So does your ability to make a full turn. If you're serious about improving, you must stay flexible. Fairway woods require a full turn of the torso and upper body without overturning the hips, to maximize distance. There are many good stretches you can do to slow down the aging process and increase flexibility! Try sitting down and resting a wood behind your neck with your hands holding the club lightly above your shoulders. Now, slowly stretch and rotate from side-to-side, turning your shoulders as close to 90 degrees as possible in relation to your hips.

2. Take a Proper Stance

Longer clubs will change your swing plane, usually making it flatter as you stand farther away from the ball. So when hitting longer clubs, particularly woods, you must focus on several things. Make sure you retain good posture. At address, flex your knees and feel as though your behind is sticking out. A good drill is to have someone hold a club along your spine. Bend forward by tilting your pelvis, and keep your back flat, not arched. This also allows your hands and arms to fall naturally from the shoulders without reaching too much for the ball. Visualize keeping the spine perpendicular to the shaft at address.

3. Watch Your Ball Position

Normally your shorter irons are played from the middle area of the stance. With fairway woods, it's a different story. Move your stance so the ball is off of the left heel (right heel for left-handed players). This allows for a greater sweeping motion as you swing. Having the ball too far back in the stance will make your approach too steep and cause you to take a divot. If you make a deep divot with a wood, it's usually because your swing is too steep.

4. "Sweep" The Ball

The proper swing arc with woods is long, wide and smooth—contrary to a short iron's arc. When hitting woods, you should feel like you are sweeping the ball from the turf and extending through the ball. The backswing should also be deeper and the follow-through extended. This means the swing arc is wider. One of the best tips to encourage this movement is to imagine striking through a ball a few inches in front of the one you are hitting. Eventually, you'll learn to hit through it—not at it!

5. Do the Waggle

A low ball flight is often caused by a closed clubface. Although this gives your shot plenty of roll, it will also hamper your ability to get the ball airborne and affect distance control. This closed-clubface problem often starts with the takeaway. Practice the waggle drill in which you fan the clubface open during the first foot or two of the backswing. This puts your hands in a good position at the top of the swing and ensures a proper wrist cock.

Lesson 13: Know Your Faults & How to Fix Them

When you get the urge to get your game in shape, make a plan and stick to it. As with golf and anything else in life, a little planning goes a long way toward success.

Work On One Drill

If you're swaying, for instance, only work on that. A common mistake many of us make is that we lose our focus. If you hit a bad shot because you lifted your head too soon, don't change your practice thoughts. Remain focused on how to avoid swaying. Otherwise, you'll go around in circles, never accomplishing anything! Continue working on one swing thought until you've perfected it. Only then should you move on to another area such as lifting the head too soon.

Practice like You're Playing

If you're at the range hitting balls, don't smash them recklessly. Practice each shot with a purpose. Remember, your time on the range should be constructive. The more real you can make it, the more valuable it becomes when you're on the course. This doesn't mean you always have to be ultra-serious. Just approach each shot as though there is a goal. This creates muscle memory and is the way all good players approach practice!

Breakdown You're Game

It's important to break down your game before every practice session. Golf can be broken down into four main areas: ball striking, short game, **mental game** and course management.

How do you rate your game in each of these areas?

When you know, devote the majority of your practice time to the weaker areas. This will benefit you in the long run.

What follows is a list of points to work on when you're practicing golf's essentials:

1. **Ball Striking**

    Most golfers spend their time working in this area. The fact is that ball striking tends to be a more important area for beginners than accomplished players. You should practice this—but not only this!

2. Short Game

The short game is comprised of chipping, pitching and putting. This is the one area where you'll be able to shave a few strokes, if you devote enough time to it. If you don't agree, just add up the strokes in an average round. Often, you'll find that more than half are spent here.

3. Mental Game

In no other sport is the mental game more important. In golf, it's just you against the course. Therefore, it's critical to learn how to deal with emotions and create positive images. Whether you're shooting your best score or your worst, emotions can affect any round. Anger can be beneficial if you channel it into positive action. Unfortunately, most people are affected negatively by it and lose concentration. How do you hold up under pressure? Find a way to approach each shot the same way. This will help you to become more consistent. This is the basis of sports psychology.

4. Course Management

Jack Nicklaus was never known for his ball-striking ability, but was able to win as a result of his golf course management. Playing smart means that you know the limitations of your game, and you are able to manage them. Play to your strengths not your weaknesses! Do you know when to go for a green and when to lay up? Understanding this facet of your game is important.

Practice A Pre-Shot Routine

The more consistent your routine before you hit a shot, the more steady your play will be. Take some time to develop a checklist or routine and keep it simple! In a short time, it will become habit—steering you toward better all-around golf.

Lesson 14: 5 Ways to 10 More Yards

How would you like to reach each par 5 on your home course in just two shots? What if you could hit a 5-iron instead of a 3-iron into a long par 4? Odds are that your game would improve. Here is a list of what I consider the five essentials to focus on if you want to hit the ball farther.

1. Widen Your Swing Arc

Tiger Woods and Davis Love are good models of long hitters with wide take-aways and big arcs. To achieve this, extend your arms as much as possible on the backswing. If you can keep your arc wide, you'll be able to create good clubhead speed without swinging any harder.

2. Lighten Your Grip Pressure

You don't have to swing hard to hit the ball a long way. In fact, this is often counterproductive and causes muscle tension. This will ultimately lead to less club head speed. After relaxing your upper body, the next key in attaining additional power is proper grip pressure. Think of your grip pressure as about a 7 on a scale of 1 to 10. Maintain this pressure throughout the swing to create good club head speed and still maintain control. If you have access to a club head speed analyzer, put your swing on it. While using the device, note the difference in your club head speed when applying tight- and relaxed-grip pressure. You'll quickly discover that the less tension you have in your body and grip pressure, the more your club head speed increases.

3. Make a Big Shoulder Turn

Jim McLean, one of the PGA's best teachers, calls shoulder turn the "X" factor. He took scientific measurements of many long hitters and found that they all have a greater shoulder than hip turn. This means that a big hip turn can actually diminish your ability to create power and club head speed because there is less torque created. Keep the lower body (the foundation) steady while the shoulder gets behind the ball, and you'll be in good shape.

4. Tuck Your Elbow

The best way to feel the proper position is to keep the right elbow tucked against your side on the downswing (left elbow for left-handed players). By doing this, you'll avoid the common error of swinging across the ball which diminishes power. Also, keeping the right elbow in delays the hit with your hands - essential in creating power and a properly timed release. When you perform the tuck correctly, the right arm (for right-handed players) is straight and your hands are not behind the ball.

5. Keep Your Knees Firm & Flexed

Think of your legs as the foundation of your swing. If your foundation is shaky and moves around too much, you'll suffer a power leak and lose ability to coil properly. Keep a firm feeling with the right knee at the top of the backswing (left knee for left-handed players) and a feeling of your weight staying on the inside of the foot. If the knee and weight move outside the foot, a sway can occur which causes numerous mechanical problems. The left knee should stay fairly still and not move laterally too much so that you maintain some width between the knees. One of our 50 beginner tips suggests that you imagine you're holding a basketball between your knees.

Lesson 15: Learning To Manage Your Game

After you've learned the fundamentals of the golf swing, the next challenge to improve your game involves proper course and game management. If you watch enough Tour events on television, you'll hear announcers talk about the importance of course and game management. All players on Tour hit the ball well and they all have solid, all-around games. Yet, only a certain percentage of them ever win. Until a Tour player learns to perfect the management of the game, the player seldom wins. For years, Jack Nicklaus was considered the best at this. Course management is best defined as playing smart golf. It's about understanding your game inside and out, your limitations, when to gamble on a shot and when to back off. The two most important areas you can manage on the course are your judgment and emotions.

To play your best, try implementing the following strategies the next time you golf:

Develop a Routine

Indecision, doubt and hesitancy lead to poor golf swings. Believe in yourself and play with confidence! Learn to accept that you'll hit bad shots and swing without that fear and pressure. Ben Hogan *(above photo)* often claimed that 90% of hitting a golf ball occurs before the swing. Take a positive approach and visualize what you want rather than what you don't want. Approach each shot as an opportunity for a great result, rather than bringing bad past experiences and fear to the shot. You'll find that maintaining the same pre-shot routine and approach every time — both mentally and physically - will help you when you're angry, nervous or feeling other strong emotions.

Control Your Emotions

Some sports reward you for getting angry or emotionally pumped up and excited. In golf, such strong emotions can hurt you unless they're properly channeled. Try to stay even-keeled, using the same approach to each shot whether you've just birdied or triple bogied. It's fine to celebrate a great shot or be angry with a poor one for a few moments. But, by the time you address your next shot, you should have the same feeling you had on the first tee.

Choose the Right Club

Before you get up there and swing away, determine the correct distance to the hole. These days, most courses have yardage markers. Make sure you take advantage of them and pay close attention to detail. Is the yardage marker's distance measured to the front or center of the green, and where is the flag in relation to that distance? This can easily be a difference of two or three clubs. Firm course conditions also affect how far you should plan for the ball to carry. In time, paying close attention helps you determine how far, on average, your shots carry. Remember to factor in trouble. Determine if there is more trouble short of the green or over it, and favor more or less club accordingly. Doing this helps to minimize your score even when you mishit the ball. Furthermore, several other factors can influence your ball's flight and carry. Remember to take wind, rain, rough and your lie into account and adjust accordingly.

Take Advantage of Tee Boxes

The only time you can change your ball's placement is when you tee it up. Take advantage of this! Always favor the same side as the trouble to get the best angle and the best percentage for avoiding it. This way, you face away, rather than into the trouble.

Weigh the Risk & Reward

If you hit a poor shot, sometimes you have to accept your "medicine" and chip out of the rough and back to the fairway. Ask yourself, what could happen if you miss the shot you are attempting? If you hit those trees you are trying to slip the ball around, will it cost you just one shot or could the decision add several more to your scorecard?

Swing With Ease

Don't try too hard to get extra distance. Forcing your swing is counterproductive because it causes a loss of balance and control. This is a mistake most amateurs make when faced with a long or difficult shot. If you can stand tall with good balance after your swing, you've probably done a good job of swinging "within" yourself. If not, choose an extra club and tone it down so that your balance is solid.

Lesson 16: Learn Seven Drills to Putt Consistently

A one-foot putt is just as important as a 300-yard drive. It's also interesting to note that you can hit every green in regulation and not score well—if your putts aren't dropping.

Putting is perhaps the most important ingredient to scoring well. On the PGA Tour, everyone hits the ball virtually the same, but the player who putts the best each week will win the tournament. Here is a list of drills to help you sink a few more putts and shave a few strokes off your score in the process:

Use the Flagstick

Most golfers have trouble keeping their putter on the proper line during the stroke. Try using a flagstick to help define the path of your putting stroke. Simply lay a flagstick flat on the putting surface and line it up with the hole. Now set the heel of your putter against the flagstick. This works as a guide when you stroke the putt. Next, pay close attention to the putter, and maintain smooth contact with the flag on both the forward and backstrokes. By doing this, you'll be able to see exactly where your stroke goes off line and correct it.

Start With a Roll

Putting a perfect, true roll on the ball starts with correct ball position. The mistake many players make is that they play the ball too far back in the stance. This causes a descending stroke and can make the ball bounce initially, rather than roll. To get the ball rolling smoothly, play the ball further up in the stance,—off the inside of your front foot. You'll notice that the proper position is under the left eye (right eye for left-handed players).

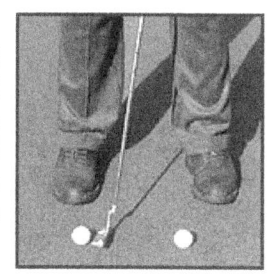

Close an Eye

Lifting the head not only hurts the full swing, but the putting stroke as well. Close the left eye (right eye for left-handed players), take a few practice strokes, and then address the ball. Doing this makes it tough to see the hole—but it's not necessary. Just focus on the ball with only the right eye (left eye for left-handed players) until you see the putter contact it. This drill trains you to keep the head and body still during the stroke.

Force a Bigger Follow-Through

Under pressure, short putts cause tension in a golfer's stroke. To maintain a good stroke, accelerate through the putt. Oftentimes, the backstroke becomes too big, causing deceleration on the forward stroke. To cure this, place a second ball about 6 inches behind the ball you're going to hit. On the backstroke, try not to strike the second ball. By restricting the backstroke, you'll force a bigger, more accelerated follow-through.

Don't Break Your Wrists

Stick a tee into the end of your putter grip. As you take your stroke, make sure that the tee stays even or slightly ahead of the **putter head** throughout the stroke. If the head passes the tee, you've probably broken your wrists and opened the door to inconsistency. On long putts, this is more difficult to do as they can require some wrist break. Therefore, use this drill for shorter, mid-range putts.

Surround the Hole

Find a hole on the practice green that has some slope. Place several balls around the hole, approximately 2 feet away. Now go around the circle, concentrating on making each putt and noticing how each putt breaks a little differently depending on its position. Challenge yourself to make each putt before graduating to moving the balls to 3 feet away. If you miss one, start again. Remember, the more you see yourself knock in these practice four-footers, the stronger your confidence will be.

Putt to a Quarter

Place a quarter on the putting green and practice putting to it. By using a smaller target, you will refine your ability to aim for and locate the center of the cup. This is also a good drill for developing the feel of speed on longer putts.

Putting is extremely important to lowering your scores. The next time you work on your game, devote as much time to putting as you do hitting balls. You'll enjoy the results.

Golf course and game management entail developing consistent habits, being aware and using common sense. Give these tips a try and watch those scores come down!

Lesson 17: Our Six Ways to Eliminate Your Slice

Playing golf with a slice, an uncontrollable shot that curves left to right, is a problem many golfers think they have to live with and accept. This isn't true—even if you've been a chronic "slicer" for years. With a little time, dedication and effort, you can learn to stop hitting stray, bending shots. Once you do, you'll start hitting the ball more consistently, add distance and achieve better control. Before long, the game will be more enjoyable.

The following is a list of quick fixes to help you hit straighter, more consistent shots:

1. Think "Topspin" & "Thumbs Up"

Watching tennis can help your golf game. All skilled tennis players apply topspin to their shots by releasing or turning over their racket when they hit the ball. In golf, the move is similar, only it's made with a club in your hand. Allowing for the release of the hands is critical to maximizing your potential and reducing slices. The next time you're practicing, take a club and swing. As you pass the impact position, think of the right hand reaching out in front on the follow through with your thumps pointing upward. This shows that the wrists rolled properly and the club was released.

2. Strengthen Your Grip

Chronic slicers have trouble getting their hands rotated through impact. Start by gripping the club in the fingers rather than the palm of your hand. At address, make sure you are able to see two or three knuckles of the left hand. This "strengthening" of the grip allows the hands to work actively.

3. Pull the Rope

Most slicers cut across the ball on the downswing. They take the club back to the outside on the backswing and cross their plane (imaginary line) to the inside on the downswing. This produces a slice. To understand the correct swing path or downswing motion, picture a rope attached to a tree above you. Now imagine yourself pulling that rope straight down. Take that thought with you to the driving range and try to pull your club straight down when starting the downswing. This also forces the right elbow to stay close to your side—a key to not crossing the line. Practicing this gives you the correct inside path and a better ability to swing out toward the target.

4. Start Back to the Inside

Imagine the line of your swing on the ground as it goes back and through toward the target. Place a range basket, or other object you don't want to break, on the ground a couple of feet behind the ball and slightly inside the intended target line. Practicing this drill forces you to swing from the inside out toward the target—the proper way!

5. Shoulders Right to Hit Left

Most players aim farther and farther to the left to accommodate their slice. This only makes matters worse by opening the shoulders. Your swing plane tends to follow your shoulders. If they are open, your odds of cutting across the ball increase. Try doing just the opposite. Aim the shoulders as far to the right as possible at address. This forces the swing to stay on the proper path.

6. Swing around Your Spine

The best way to eliminate the typical slice, one that is caused by a reverse pivot or sway motion, is to swing your spine and finish around and to the left. Use "x-ray vision"—picture your spine remaining in a near-perpendicular angle to the ground at all times during the swing. Now, just swing around the center of it!

These tips work best if they're combined with each other. For instance, achieving the proper swing path won't prevent you from hitting to the right if you don't use your hands properly.

Practice each strategy separately in the beginning and then combine them. You'll soon be saying goodbye to your slice—forever!

Lesson 18: Playing From Various Bunker Lies

When attempting a bunker shot, most amateurs know to twist their feet into the sand. This is a good idea, but how you should do this varies depending on the lie. Ignoring different types of lies and ball positions in the sand sets you up for poor balance, slipping and an inability to control ball flight—not to mention higher scores!

Consistently practice the following footwork basics and watch your sand play become more predictable:

Ball below Feet: Use Less Lower Body

This is perhaps the toughest position because there is a tendency to fall forward during the swing and change your spine angle. Dig your heels into the slope and try to feel as though the weight is on the balls of your feet. You'll need a little more knee flex to keep you from topping the ball. Try to maintain the same amount of flex throughout the swing. Remember less is better when it comes to using leg and lower-body action—especially on this difficult shot!

Downhill Lies: Set Your Weight

Gravity forces most of your weight on the downhill or lower leg. Make sure to set your weight on the inside of the forward foot for more stability. I also recommend that you turn out your toe slightly to help absorb the extra weight transfer caused by gravity. Normally, you would open your stance considerably in the sand. However, on these shots, you have to be careful. If you open the stance, your right leg will be in the way of your swing. To avoid this, pull your back foot away a few inches.

Uphill Lies: Brace Yourself

With gravity working to keep your weight on the downhill leg, it's important to brace it firmly into the sand. Angle your leg into the slope so that the weight is on the inside of the downhill leg. When you swing, the weight will be easier to shift forward.

Ball above Feet: Adjust Your Aim

The first adjustment to make is to dig your toes in deeper than your heels. This helps keep you level and makes it easier to remain balanced. Keep the legs flexed. Aiming a bit to the right and using a slightly open stance is also recommended, as uphill lies tend to promote a hook or pulled shot.

Buried Lie: Use the Right Twist

The deeper you submerge your feet into the sand, the deeper the club enters the sand. Therefore, if the ball is only slightly buried, you don't need to twist in too deep. For a severely buried lie, twisting in to the approximate depth of the buried lie helps you get under the ball. For this type of shot, you need to pick up the club steeply and hit down and through on a sharp U-like swing plane.

Obviously, the best advice is to stay out of these tough lies in the first place. But we all know that's easier said than done. Besides, this game wouldn't be any fun if it weren't challenging!

Lesson 19: Learning to Properly Release the Club

Many players have shared common problems—the inability to generate power and slicing the ball. In most instances, both of these problems stem from having a poor or improper release. This lesson lists ways to help you release or turn over the club.

Whether you want to gain a few extra yards or are just beginning and want to ingrain proper habits, put the following tips to work for better all-around ball striking:

Try a Split Grip

Perhaps the best drill to emphasize proper hand release is to grip the club so that you have a few inches of space between your hands. Next, make a few swings with the club going only half way back and through. Practicing this drill helps exaggerate the feeling of the right hand crossing over the left. When you do this properly, you'll see the toe of the club facing upward, both at hip height on the backswing and at hip height on the follow-through.

Don't Hold On

"Holding on" means that instead of being relaxed through impact, there is a tendency to grip too tightly and hold on—not releasing the full potential of the swing. When you anticipate the hit rather than swinging through the ball, there is inevitably a tendency to tighten and hold on too much. The most fluid way to swing is as though you aren't hitting the ball at all, but rather swinging through it.

Ben Hogan once remarked, "Ninety percent of a golf shot—good or bad—occurs before the swing." Start by standing very erect with your back flat. Flex the knees and push your behind out so that your knees are roughly above the balls of the feet. Try to maintain this position as you bend over from the waist. Think of the arms and hands being low and relaxed as though gravity is pulling them straight down. Now stand at address with a club. Make sure that an angle is established with the wrists. This angle is important because you are lessening the moving parts of your swing by setting the wrist cock in advance. This allows for a hinging action of the wrists and makes it much easier to release the club on the follow-through. Quite often, beginner golfers reach too much for the ball. This causes the wrists to roll in the swing, rather than hinge and unhinge.

Relax Your Grip Pressure

Start by determining your grip pressure. How tight are you gripping the club on a scale of 1-10, with 10 being as tight as you can squeeze and 1 being not holding on at all? Generally, the best players grip about a 6 on this scale. Any tighter and tension gets in the way, going all the way up the arms and into the upper body. Too much grip tension inhibits the lag (delayed hit) and release motions that are critical to extension and a full release of the hands and arms. After you have set a light but firm pressure, monitor the consistency throughout the swing. Is it the same throughout, or does it tighten or loosen somewhere during the swing? Keeping a light pressure consistently allows you the freedom to make the correct move. Remember, the tighter you grip the club, the less your hands work in unison, and the more they inhibit your release.

Develop a Pre-Shot Routine

Being tight in the body and with the grip aren't the only things that affect your game and release. Your mind must also remain clear and focused. Start by using a consistent pre-shot routine. This routine should allow you to relax and visualize positive results. Developing a pre-shot routine can clear the mind so you're free to go ahead and give the ball your best shot.

Drop the Right Foot Back

Dropping the right foot back as you take some swings helps you to swing along a path that allows for a full hand release. Drop the right foot back about one foot at address, and try to swing across your body with easy swings. After you get the feeling of your hands being able to release, trick yourself—retain the motion while slowly moving the foot back into the normal position.

Use the Big Muscles

To generate your full power potential, you must use your trunk and midsection. Any athlete, from boxer to baseball pitcher, will agree that their power starts from the legs, trunk and midsection. This is where the big muscles are located and where you must rely for a smoother motion. Practice feeling that the belly button is facing the target at the end of the swing and that you finish the swing balanced on the right toe. To fully release the hips, weight must get off the left foot and up onto the toe. If you make a good body release combined with the hand release, you'll wonder where all that power was stored!

One of the biggest breakthroughs you will feel in golf is when your body and hands release their energy at the same time. When this is happening, the right elbow stays close to the right side—almost touching the hip—as both it and the hips move or release through that poor golf ball. This is called efficient use of energy and it comes only through practice.

Lesson 20: Learn To Transfer Your Weight

It seems like it should be easy: Start the swing with the weight evenly distributed on both feet and finish with it on the left foot and right toe. After all, we do this every time we take a step and in almost any sport. Proper weight transfer is necessary to powerfully propel an object. Yet, many golfers often try to help the ball get up in the air by hitting up or at it.

The following lesson will help you understand some of the ways to hit through the ball with a correct weight shift:

Understand Weight Shift

Students often find it hard to understand and feel their weight shift. A good way to begin is to close your eyes and take a few practice swings. Afterwards, give each foot a percentage weighting for the beginning at address, middle and end of the swing. If you're swinging properly, the beginning or address position should feel like your weight is evenly distributed between your left and right feet on a flat lie. At the top of the backswing, if you've made a good turn without swaying, it should feel like 80% of your weight is on the inside of your right foot and 20% is on the inside of your left foot. The follow-through should feel exactly the opposite.

If these closed-eye swings aren't close to these numbers, try the following drills:

Walk Through the Shot

Take your normal address position and swing a club to the top of the **backswing.** As you come down and through the ball, make an effort to step forward after you've made contact, as if you are walking. Gary Player made this move famous and still does it on many shots. This drill and position emphasizes that you've made a good weight shift.

You "Can" Do It

Place an object such as a soda can about a foot behind your ball. Using a short-iron, try to hit your ball without hitting the can. You'll notice that you're forced to come down at a steeper angle. By swinging with this steeper angle, you're also forced to shift properly off the right foot and take a divot in front of the ball. When you don't, you'll find yourself hitting behind the ball or topping it. This is often the result of hanging back on the right foot. After a few swings, try placing that same object in front of the ball about 2 feet. The goal is to swing out over the can as low as possible on the follow-through without actually hitting it. This extension drill promotes a strong weight shift to the left leg and gets you to hit through, rather than at, your ball. This is great if you often top the ball.

Swing On a Slope

To feel weight shift happening naturally, try swinging while standing on a downhill or uphill slope. On a downhill slope, gravity pushes your weight toward the front foot, making it easier to finish the swing with the weight fully transferred. When doing this, keep your shoulder line fairly parallel with the slope of the ground to avoid hitting behind the ball.

Keep Your Weight Inside

Keeping your weight on the inside of the right foot during the backswing is critical to shifting properly. Allowing the weight to get to the outside of the foot doesn't give you a strong base to push off from when "springing" over to the left side. This can also lead to the dreaded sway. This results in a lot of wasted movement and is detrimental to good swing mechanics. To find a proper position, keep the right knee over the inside of the foot at address and throughout the backswing. Obviously, it's not helpful to think about this during the swing. However, stop at the top of the swing occasionally and check your position. In time, this will pay off in added power and more solid hits.

There are many more ways to drill the concept of weight shifting inside. However, you must first learn how it feels and start noticing what's going on throughout your swing. After you can do that, you will see the correlation between solid shots and good shifting. This is how the pros make it look so easy, yet hit it so far. Also try getting that right toe of your golf shoe dirty. This is a good sign of fully shifting and turning.

As always, don't forget to have fun!

Lesson 21: Learn to Check Your Alignment

When it comes to fundamentals, you'll often hear about grip, posture and ball position. Although all of these are important to building a consistent swing, alignment is the most critical. You can have the best swing in the world. However, if you're not properly aligned with the target, you'll hit the ball anywhere.

Imagine trying to sink a pool ball in the pocket without aiming. You'd really have to manipulate that pool cue on the forward stroke in order to get the ball on line wouldn't you? The same is true in golf, so why make a difficult game more complex?

The majority of amateurs align too far to the right, setting themselves up for the familiar "over-the-top" swing in an effort to get the ball on line. The result is usually a pull, a slice, or glancing contact with the ball.

The main alignment check points are the feet, knees, hips and shoulders. Unless you're making a conscious effort to draw or fade the ball, these points should all be consistent and parallel to the target line.

Start Behind the Ball

The first step in your pre-shot routine is to get directly behind the ball and draw an imaginary line from your ball to your target. Although you'll see most pros do this on TV, you will seldom see amateurs taking this approach. This allows you to get a good sense of target and to visualize a positive ball flight.

Square the Clubface to the Target

Pick a spot such as a leaf or divot in front of the ball that's on the same imaginary target line you saw when you stood behind the ball. As you set up, align the clubface perpendicular to that spot. Another way is to line up the label on the ball toward the target and then the clubface. Check yourself often, as this is an area that requires a great deal of precision.

Place Clubs on the Ground

One of the most effective ways to train proper alignment is to place 2 clubs in a parallel position on the ground. Start by aiming the first club directly at the flag and another parallel to it, approximately where your feet would be. Laying clubs on the ground is also a great way to spot-check how you're doing. If you set up in what you think is the correct position and lay down the clubs once in a while, it will allow you to catch poor habits early. Remember, if the feet are to the right of the target, you'll have a harder time clearing the left hip and using the legs properly. This drill ensures perfect aim.

Check Your Shoulder Position

As you look back and forth toward the flag—verifying your aim—there's a tendency to leave the shoulders open. This will prove counterproductive to an otherwise good position. To check this last area, try placing a club on the line of the shoulders with the grip end facing the flag. If you extend the line of where the grip is pointing, you'll get a good indication of direction. By doing this, you can also ensure the shoulder line is pointing in the same direction as the line on which your feet are aimed.

As you can see, alignment is imperative. Without it, you could swing and hit the ball like Tiger Woods, but never make a birdie or hit a green.

Lesson 22: Adopting Proper Putting Fundamentals

After seeing numerous putting styles, we have come to the conclusion that the majority of great golfers use the same putting fundamentals. Some of these are physical and some are mental. Very little of the so-called "magic" actually comes from a putter, but rather from the confidence within the player.

Think Positive

Positive thinking can represent the doorway to good putting. Remember a time when you were putting well. It probably felt as though you couldn't miss, and you had a greater belief that the ball would go in. Positive feelings and visualization are the key. This belief comes from prior success and success comes from solid fundamentals and practice.

Grip for Success

Hold the hands close enough together so that they work as a unit, rather than independently. When they're separate, there's a better chance of the wrists breaking down, which leads to inconsistency. A popular grip used by many tour players is a reverse overlap that takes the forefinger of the left hand off the putter and rests it on the little finger of the right hand. A cross-handed grip is also worth trying if you break the wrists during the stroke. Equally important is grip pressure. Aim for light pressure rather than tight pressure because tightness diminishes feel.

Consider Ball Position

The left eye should be directly over the ball at address. This means that the ball is placed forward in the stance, off the inside of the left foot. This also gives you a much better perspective of your putt's intended line of travel.

Keep the Putter Moving

Accelerate the putter toward the hole. Practice some short putts about one foot from the hole and try rolling the ball and putter right over the hole. Remember, the follow-through should exceed the backstroke. You can ensure this by placing another ball behind the ball you're hitting on the practice green. As you make the backstroke, stop when you hit the second ball.

Have the Right Distance

Standing too far from the ball causes an improper stroke path—one that makes too much of an arc from the inside so that it's difficult for the face to be square to the target. Conversely, if you stand too close, you tend to force the backstroke outside of the target line. When making these mistakes, it forces you to manipulate the putter to square it at impact.

Locate the Hands Ahead

Locating your hands forward is another fundamental common to good putting techniques. If your hands are behind the ball, there's a tendency to add loft to the putt and break your wrists. By keeping your hands up front and even with the ball or slightly ahead, you'll ensure a better roll.

Lock the Body

Keep body movement minimal. Good players putt while keeping their bodies locked in position for the entire stroke. Doing this allows the shoulders, rather than the hips, to dominate the movement. A great way to check how solid you are is to use the sun's shadow. Putt with the shadow facing in front of you so you can detect any lateral movement. Place a ball or club on the green at the outer edges of the shadow of your hips. As you take some practice strokes, pay attention and see if you can detect any movement. You can also practice this shadow trick to ensure your head and shoulders stay in place and don't sway.

If you can blend these key fundamental with your own style, you'll find that your putts will start to fall more frequently.

Lesson 23: Getting Your Total Game in Shape

Playing good golf involves a lot more than just beating around countless balls on the driving range. If you really want to get the most from the sport, you must concentrate your efforts on several key areas that help make your game complete and keep you on track.

Let's explore the following areas that have the biggest impact on your game:

Practice Makes Perfect

There is no point investing in swing instruction if you can't learn to repeat what you learned. Remember, a golf teacher is only responsible for part of the picture. Repetition breeds confidence and confidence breeds success. There is no substitute for practice. Practice must be performed with purpose and then complemented with play.

Get Professional Instruction

Receiving professional instruction on a regular basis is vital to keeping your game on track. So often, we think we can solve our game problems without help. This can sometimes result in making a simple problem worse. A check up by a golf instructor can make a huge difference. Remember, a well-trained professional eye can see things that you can't.

Get Out There & Do It

Playing the game of golf is what it's all about. It's hard to perfect your technique and implement all the advice you read, unless you get on the course often. Practice and play with purpose and measure the results.

Think Positive

This is often an overlooked part of the game even though it accounts for so much. Listen to the **self-talk in your head**. Are you hard on yourself? Do you adopt a "poor me" attitude? When you really listen to your inner self, you'll be amazed at what you hear. Try to maintain a positive outlook while on the course. The more confident your thoughts are, the more confident your play. Before long, your scores will drop. Golf may be one of the greatest games ever devised—it combines all the elements of balance and strength with both body and mind.

The Right Stuff

Who needs custom clubs? An easy response would be "everyone." However, certain players tend to reap greater rewards than others by using custom clubs. These players commonly have unique body features. For example, they might have short or long fingers, a tall body with relatively short arms, or a short body with relatively long arms. Everyone is unique. Remember, don't adjust your game to a set of clubs—adjust your clubs to your game.

Fit Your Game

Compose the set of the clubs you are most efficient using. There's no point carrying a 2-iron if you can't get it up in the air and don't feel confident using it. Instead, opt for a 5 or 7-wood. Many Senior Tour and women professionals do this. Even players such as Nick Faldo have been seen carrying high-lofted fairway woods in their bag. Because the rules allow for 14 clubs only, fill your bag with ones you use most often and most efficiently.

If taking your game up a notch is important to you, review this short list and make sure you give each area appropriate attention. The results could take you up to the next level!

Lesson 24: Getting Out Of Trouble Spots

During the course of a round, you'll often find yourself in situations that require specialty shots to get out of trouble. Most of the time, a hook or slice can be the worst thing in the world. However, there may be times when you need to deliberately hit such a shot. In fact, the ability to choose your type of shot depending on the situation is what transforms average golfers into great golfers. This lesson describes different types of shots and the easiest ways to hit them:

Hook

For right-handed golfers, a hook curves from right to left. This shot tends to roll farther than a sliced shot. To hit a hook, the clubface must be closed in relation to the target line at impact. The simplest way to hit this shot is to start with a normal stance and grip, and direct the clubface toward the target. Then pull back the right or back foot a few inches, so that the line of your feet is aiming to the right of the target 10-15 yards. Aligning your feet this way forces you to swing on an inside-to-outside plane. At impact, this swing path puts a counterclockwise spin on the ball and makes it hook. This technique coupled with a closed clubface produces an even bigger hook. If you're having trouble, ensure there's a feeling of the hands rolling over through impact. For a more pronounced hook, manipulate your grip. Rotate your hands more to the right at address.

Slice

You can hit a slicing shot many ways. The simplest way to slice on purpose is to reverse the procedure you followed for the hook. Pull the left foot back so your stance points to the left. Leave the clubface pointed toward the target and swing across on the new feet line. You can add more slice by "weakening" the grip. Rotate the hands and grip position to the left. When you hit a slice, there's less hand action and rotation through the ball.

Fade & Draw

A fade is a mild version of a slice and a draw is a mild version of a hook. Because hitting the ball dead straight every time is so difficult, good players incorporate slight nuances of the hook or slice; they attempt to make one of these ball flights their "bread & butter" shot. This way, they know the direction the ball is curving, allowing for greater control and course management. Jack Nicklaus has always said the best way to hit a fade is to slightly open your clubface at address and take a normal swing. To hit a draw, slightly close the clubface at address and take your usual swing.

High Shot

Hitting high shots can be valuable in situations where the greens are very firm or you need to get the ball over a high object such as a tree. This type of shot lands softer, allowing golfers to carry over bunkers and still keep the ball close to the flag. Start by placing the ball slightly more forward in the stance than normal. Then visualize your spine angle being vertical to the ground at address. When you approach impact on the swing, your spine angle can be at a slightly upward or "launch" angle. You achieve this best by ensuring your head stays back through the shot. It's OK to shift the weight of your lower body, but force your upper body to stay back. A more upright swing plane promotes a higher ball flight.

Low Shot

Low shots are fun to hit, especially into wind or under trees. Place the ball farther back in the stance compared to your normal ball position. As you come through impact, there are two positions to feel. First, make sure that the hands have stayed in front of the ball, keeping the loft of the club low. Second, ensure the spine angle is still vertical rather than a typical launch angle. A shorter backswing often helps here as well. This position gives you a nice controlled low shot. The shot tends to roll more, so plan accordingly.

These are just a few of the many creative shots you can learn to produce in an imaginative round of golf.

Lesson 25: The Art of the Bump & Run

As the old saying goes, there are many ways to get the ball in the hole. While this is certainly true, the majority of good players realize that specific types of shots are more effective and consistent than others. Conventional wisdom indicates that it's best not to loft the ball any more than necessary. Nonetheless, many players insist on hitting lofted or lob shots when they aren't necessary. These lofted shots are much more difficult to control than the good old "bump and run."

If you have ever watched the British Open, you have certainly seen a bump and run. A bump and run is a shot that lands over the fringe less than a third of the way to the hole and then rolls or "runs" the rest of the way. This shot is ideal in windy, firm conditions or when no bunkers are guarding the front of the green. On shorter distances, it's almost as though you are "bumping" the ball gently onto the putting surface and letting it run the rest of the way. Both club selection and technique are important in pulling off this shot.

Practice This Drill

One of the biggest destroyers of consistency around the green is overuse of the wrists. When they break down through impact, it opens the door to a chipping nightmare. For the bump and run (and nearly all shots around the green), position the hands slightly in front of the ball at address. The hands should also reach impact in this position and through to the finish. To aid in this, play the ball slightly back of the middle of your stance.

A good way to ensure the correct hand position is to have a friend place the grip end of a club slightly in front of the ball as you begin your downswing. As you swing, let your club hit the grip end of the club on the ground, stopping your forward progress. This forces your hands to stay ahead of the ball.

Position the Shaft on Your Wrist

Grip your club all the way down—below the grip and on the shaft—so there's enough of the grip above your hands to rest it on your left forearm as you simulate the address position. In this position, your club will be well above the ground, so you can't hit the ball. Now, take some practice strokes. If the club's grip stays connected to the left forearm on the follow-through of your pretend chip shot, it's good. If it slips off your forearm, it's an indication there's too much wrist use. Do this until you can keep the grip from disconnecting.

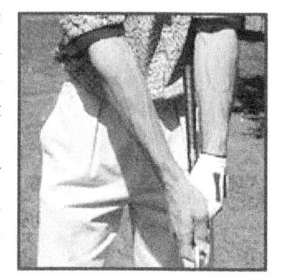

Pick the Right Stick

Many players use the same club for all low-trajectory shots. This isn't the most effective method. For more predictability, you should change clubs depending on the lie, the slope, green speed and various other factors. That way, you can use the same stroke every time—only changing the loft of the club, rather than having to change the technique for each shot. Good club selection also requires imagination; you should make it a priority to visualize each shot before you attempt it. Picture where you want the ball to land (always in the first third of the green with two thirds being in roll), and then choose the club that will give the desired loft.

Practice the low-trajectory shot on a flat area. Use the same stroke on every shot while alternating clubs—6-iron all the way down to a pitching wedge. Pay close attention to how high the ball goes and how much roll each club produces.

Point Your Watch toward the Target

This is an old drill that really works. Simply imagine the back of the left wrist or your watch facing the target. As you follow through, keep the face of your watch directed at the target. It will be natural for it to turn over to the left or face upward as you go through the ball. However, resist and keep pointing that wrist toward the target—and toward better chipping.

Bad Shots in Golf

For a high-handicap golfer, hitting bad shots is quite common. This is understandable since inexperienced golfers don't have a sound swing. With practice, the bad shots will eventually disappear. Some players will eradicate these bad shots very quickly, whereas others may take longer. Identifying bad shots and what causes them can hasten your quest to eliminate them.

A bad shot is a shot whose behavior is not what you wanted. The main cause of hitting a bad shot is incorrect contact of the clubface with your ball.

Here are some common bad shots:

Fat Shot

A fat shot occurs when your clubhead hits the ground before hitting the ball. The ground slows down your swing speed considerably. Your ball flies into the air for a short while and then drops quickly to the ground.

Try to change the position of your ball in your stance. Usually you can gauge the position with some practice swings made near the ball. Stand in a position that will allow you to hit the ball first instead of the ground.

Shank Shot

This is a really bad shot. A shank is where the side of your club hits the ball instead of the clubface. This happens when you sent your clubhead too far away from your body. The shank is a dangerous shot because the ball takes off at a right angle towards you. You can get hit by your own ball!

To cure the shank shot, try standing further from the ball. A slower and more relaxed swing will also help.

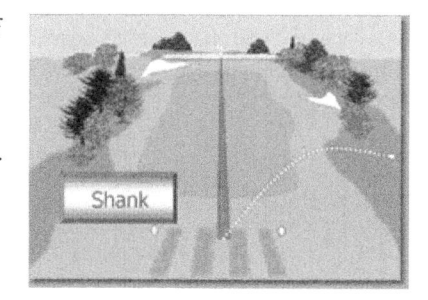

Slice Shot

The slice is a very common bad shot for beginners. Your ball travels from left to right, traveling farther and farther away from your target. A slice is caused by an open clubface resulting from an out-to-in swing.

An immediate cure is to close your clubface slightly at address. This will compensate the out-to-in swing. A better way is to correct your out-to-in swing by keeping your right arm closer to your body during the downswing.

Hook Shot

The hook is the opposite of the slice. Your ball travels from right to left, moving farther and farther left of the target. The cause is the opposite of the slice; your swing travels in an in-to-out direction resulting in a closed clubface upon contact with the ball. A hook shot rolls more than a slice shot. If you consistently hit a hook shot, try hitting a slice. This may compensate for your hook.

Fade Shot

A mild form of the slice is the fade. A fade isn't actually a bad shot because it's controllable. Many golfers, including pros, often play this shot intentionally.

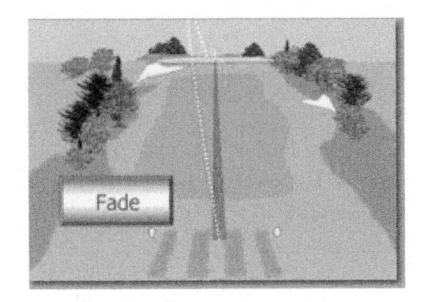

Push Shot

A push shot is a straight shot that travels to the right of the target instead of toward it. The direction of your swing causes this shot. You contact the ball squarely, but your swing isn't along the target line. Make sure your clubface travels along the target line to eliminate the push shot.

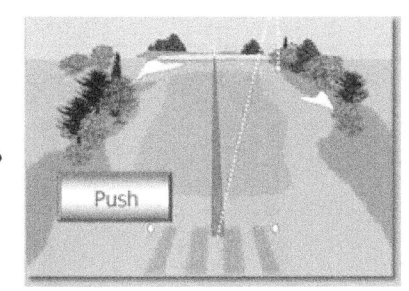

Pull Shot

The opposite of the push shot is the pull shot. Your ball flies straight to the left of the target. Again, the cause is the direction of your swing. The cure is to swing along the target line.

Top Shot

A top shot is when the ball hardly leaves the ground. This happens when your clubface contacts the top of the ball. To cure a top shot, concentrate on hitting the back of the ball. Shifting your weight to the front will also help.

Sometimes, when a ball is hit near the top, it may fly at a few feet above the ground for a considerable distance and then continue to roll. This shot is called a "worm burner".

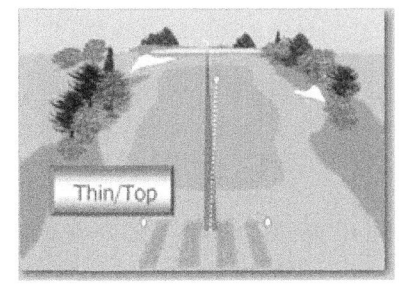

Chili-Dip

A fat shot hit near the green is called a chili-dip. As always, keep your eyes focused on the ball when you are near the green.

Overswinging

One of the factors leading to inconsistency is the overswing. Overswinging occurs when you swing your club back and over your head to a point where your shaft is beyond parallel to the ground at the top of your backswing.

This usually happens when you try to muscle a shot in an attempt to drive the ball farther.

Overswinging becomes a problem when one part of your body is out of synch with the others. This makes it difficult to bring the club back to the proper place in time. You may not able to repeat the same movement consistently.

However, if you can hit the ball squarely like this, you should continue.

The keyword is consistency. Tom Watson and Nancy Lopez are just two professionals who perform well with their huge swing.

If overswinging is a problem, try to identify the cause and correct it. This can be done by standing in front of a mirror or with the help of a professional instructor.

At the top of your backswing, make sure:

- Your weight is over to your right leg
- Your right knee is flexed
- Your left arm is not severely bent at the elbow
- Your spine angle is not tilted toward the target
- The fingers of your left hand are closed
- The butt end of your club is in contact with the edge of your left hand
- Your wrists are not over-hinged
- You can see the ball with both eyes

If you pass all of the above criteria, you can't overswing.

More Short Game Tips

The short game makes up more than 70% of golf, hence we spend a bit more time on it. Driving the ball is fun, but the real talent shows when you are less than 100 yards from the pin.

Below are the components of the short game:

Pitching

A pitch shot is used to send the ball on the green at a distance from 40- 90 yards.

Here are the steps:

1. Stand with a slightly open stance with the ball towards your right foot.
2. Keep your left arm straight and in front of the ball.
3. Your weight should be on your left side all the time.
4. Make a smooth, full swing initiated by your arms, not your lower body.
5. Keep your shoulders square and your left arm straight.
6. Flex your right knee towards the target.
7. Maintain the back of your left hand facing the target for a longer period.
8. Your follow-through should be a mirror-image of your backswing.

The aim of a pitch shot is to land on the green with as little roll as possible.

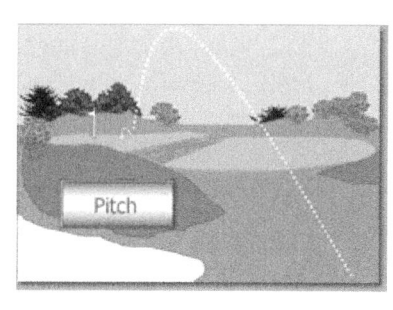

Chipping

When your ball is less than 40 yards, a chip shot is used. Basically, there are two ways of chipping your ball onto the green:

Bump & Run – a ball that flies low, bumps on the green and runs a long way. You can use nearly the entire range of irons, depending on the flag location.

- Use an open stance
- Play the ball way back
- Hood the clubface to slightly reduce its loft
- Use a putting arm and shoulder movement
- Strike downward, hitting the ball and ground at the same time
- Sweep through the ball along the target line
- Follow through and keep your eyes on the ball

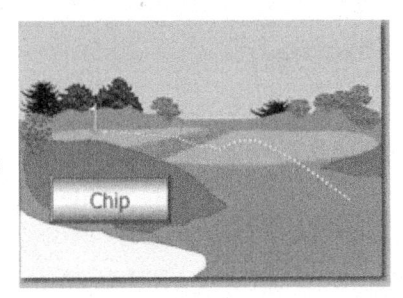

Flop Shot – a ball that flies high and lands with little roll. When there is water or a bunker in front of the green, a flop shot is used. Use a sand wedge or lob wedge (60%) for this shot.

- Start with an open stance
- Ball position should be at the middle or slightly ahead of middle of stance
- Open up your clubface and aim at the target
- Swing your arms lazily along your body line
- Slide the clubface under the ball keeping the clubface facing the sky
- Keep your arms moving through the shot

The key to a successful flop is a slow and easy tempo. Trying the flop on a hardpan is risky.

Getting the Chip Shot Right

The two most common mistakes when chipping is the fat-shot that drops a few feet in front of you (called a chili-dip), and the thin clip that sends your ball shooting right across the green (called a skull shot).

In your determined effort to get your club under the ball, you strike the ground first. Because this is a delicate shot, you try to finesse it with a slow, decelerated stroke. The speed of your clubhead is so slow you can't even plow through the ground to lift up the ball.

On the other hand, you miss the ground completely or you brush the grass and hit the ball almost at mid center with your clubhead on its way up. This will shoot the ball up low and at a fast pace. The ball will probably fly beyond your target and over the green.

To avoid these two mistakes, you need to strike the ball first, then the ground. Getting a clean contact isn't easy, but it's not really difficult either.

There are two important things to keep in mind. The first is your point of contact. You need to strike the ball below its equator on your downswing. This requires concentration and focus. Many beginners are so anxious to see where their ball is heading that they turn their head at the crucial moment. You must watch where your club strikes the ball. Although the motion is too fast for your eyes, remain focused on that spot.

The next important factor is acceleration. This may appear to be a contradiction. You may believe that accelerating the club will send the ball shooting past the green. All because this is supposed to be a delicate shot.

You need to hit down at the ball. You need to hit a short shot, and you need to accelerate the clubhead. You can accomplish all of this with a short backswing.

Many golfers find it difficult to conceptualize the short backswing. They're so used to swinging their clubhead back beyond shoulder height that a clubhead at waist height may seem short. When they swing their club at waist level and then accelerate, they'll probably send the ball more than 20 yards. When faced with a distance of less than 15 yards, the only solution is to slow down their swing.

Many golfers also want to send their balls high when chipping. Unless there's a bunker in front of the green, you don't need to chip the ball high. The purpose of a high chip is to send the ball over something.

A better shot to use is a low chip shot. Observe the pros on TV. If the flag is less than 20 yards and there is a clear path, you will notice them chipping low and running the ball to the hole.

The next time you're at the practice range, try to chip a low running shot by using a short backswing. Remember to accelerate you clubhead toward impact. Keep this accelerated swing constant. The distance the ball runs will now depend on the distance of your backswing.

You will be on your way to what they call 'one chip one putt'. With a little bit of luck, you may not even need to putt!

One Club vs. One Swing

The chip shot is usually played from a distance of less than 40 yards to the green. This shot requires a delicate touch. There are two schools of thought on achieving it – the one-club method and the one-swing method.

The one-club method utilizes one club for all chip shots. The golfer varies his swing speed to send the ball various distances. The one-swing method utilizes one swing. The golfer uses different clubs to send the ball different distances.

You can practice both methods and then decide which one you prefer.

One-Club Method

1. Set up a test target 10 yards away.
2. Chip 20 balls at the target using an 8-iron.
3. Repeat with 9-iron through sand wedge or your highest lofted club, chipping 20 balls for each club.
4. Decide which club is most comfortable. This is your approach chip club. Keep the others in the bag.
5. Practice 30-50 balls with this club at the 10-yard target.
6. Set yourself a passing percentage. 70% is reasonably good.
7. If you pass, increase the distance to 20 yards.
8. Repeat with 10-yard increments until you reach the maximum distance you can chip.

One-Swing Method

1. Set up a test target 30 yards away.
2. Using your most consistent and comfortable half-swing and a 9-iron, hit 2-3 balls towards the target.
3. If your 9-iron falls short, change to a longer iron. If you overshoot, change to a shorter iron.
4. Once you have found the iron to reach your test target, keep the others in your bag.
5. Practice 30-50 balls with this club at the test target.
6. Set a passing percentage or 70% or higher.
7. Once you are hitting the mark consistently, this is your swing method.
8. Practice with other clubs and note the distance of each club.
9. You should not only reach the distance, but also consistently hit the target at that distance.

Sand Play

Sooner or later, you will find yourself in the sand bunker. Actually, bunkers shots are easier than you think. This is one time you don't even have to hit the ball. You are hitting the sand behind the ball which gives you a bigger margin of error!

Here is how you do it:

- Choose the sand wedge for a greenside bunker.
- Gauge your distance from the target.
- Plant your feet firmly. Wriggling your feet into the sand will give you an idea of its firmness.
- Use an open stance. Taking the target line as 12 o'clock, your feet should line up at 11 o'clock.
- Offset your clubface to 1 o'clock to counter your open stance.
- Open your clubface to face the sky as in the flop shot. For wet or hard sand, square your stance and close your clubface.
- Swing along your body line keeping your body still.
- Your club must strike the sand 2-3 inches behind the ball. The less sand you take, the more spin you put on the ball. Less sand also means greater risk.
- Keep your wrists firm throughout and well after impact.
- A steep downswing angle will yield a shorter distance, while a shallow angle will hit the ball longer.

The above instructions are for a normal sand shot. However, your ball may end up in some tricky situations. Such conditions may call for a slight variation.

Below are some possible scenarios:

- **In A Footprint** – You find your ball inside a footprint left by someone else. The solution is to play the ball as a **lob shot**. You may need to switch to a pitching wedge or a 9-iron.
- **In A Downhill Lie** – Your ball is lying at the back of the bunker in a downhill position. You need to take more sand at the back of the ball. Close the clubface more to suit the contour. Play the ball off your right heel to promote a steeper entry angle.
- **In An Uphill Lie** – Your ball is in front of the bunker in an uphill lie. Since the terrain is uphill, your club will dig deeper into the sand. In this situation, hit closer to the ball with a stronger follow-through. Play an out-to-in cut shot. Your clubface should remain open and square to the line of flight.
- **On Top Of Firm Level Sand With No Overhanging Lip** – This is a rare situation. Use your putter and a flat-arm motion to keep your clubhead parallel to the sand. Keep your body weight on your left foot.

Buried Bunker Lie – If the sand is soft, the ball may become embedded.

If you are thinking of a bigger swing with a bigger follow-through, you'll be in big trouble. The laws of the usual bunker shot don't apply to this situation.

Here is what you should do:

- Your stance should be a bit squarer than the usual bunker stance.
- The clubface should also be squarer.
- Have a steep backswing.
- Strike the leading edge of the clubface into the sand 1-3 inches behind the ball. You can swing hard.
- Do NOT follow through.

The ball will pop out of the sand with little or no spin.

"Knowing the basics of sand play takes away your fear; knowing the subtleties will actually lead you to enjoy playing from bunkers."

– Greg Norman

Putting

Hole	1	2	3	4	5	6	7	8	9	Total
Par	4	5	4	4	3	5	3	4	4	36
Driver	1	1	0	1	0	1	0	1	1	6
Long Irons	1	1	1	0	1	1	1	0	1	7
Mid Irons	0	1	1	1	0	1	0	1	1	6
Short Irons	1	1	0	1	1	2	1	1	0	8
Putter	2	2	2	2	2	1	2	2	2	17

The table above indicates how many times a typical bogey player used his clubs during the first 9 holes of his round. A glance at his putter usage reveals him to be a skilled putter. He never one three-putted which is a feat even the pros would admire.

In the round of 9 holes, this golfer used his putter 17 times. This is more than twice the number of times he used any other equipment! This shows how important putting is to the game of golf. Therefore, it makes sense to invest time in this aspect of the game. Many golfers spend time at the range practicing their driving and irons, but they don't spend serious time on the practice green.

Putting is called a game within a game because the skills involved are different from the rest of the game. Putting really lives up to the adage "Drive for show; Putt for dough". You can have the most spectacular drive in the round. However, that's not going to show in the scorecard.

If your putting is no good, you will probably end up buying the beers!

Here are five simple steps to help you become a better putter:

1. Position – Stand in a position so that your eyes are over the line of putt. Your left eye should be directly over the ball. To test if this is done correctly, hold the putter loosely and directly under your eyes and let it hang straight down. As you look down, does the putter cover the ball? If not, move forward or backward.
Now that your ball is directly under your left eye, your hands should remain a little forward of the ball. The putter shaft should be aligned with your left forearm. This gives a good roll to the ball.

2. Grip – The putting stroke is done with no wrist movement. Your hands, arms and shoulder should work together as a unit. Let your shoulder direct the movement of the club. Grip the club lightly to promote a better feel.

3. Aim – Find a target to aim your ball. If the hole is close enough and the ground is level, make it your target. If the hole is on a slope, the target should be the point where your ball will make its turn. This is called the apex. Imagine a straight line from there to the middle of your putter.

Unlike the full swing, your leg alignment is not as important in putting. What is important is your putter face remaining square to the target line. This is the line your putter should follow.

4. Stroke – You putting stroke involves only your shoulders and arms. Forget about the rest of the body. Keep them as still as possible, especially your head. Focus on contacting the ball when your swing is ascending to encourage a more forward roll. A forward rolling ball stays on line longer.

5. Acceleration – The purest stroke in putting is the pendulum stroke. The backswing and follow-through are of equal length. Deceleration is the worst enemy of putting. Stroke through the ball, not at it.

Nerves are the next biggest enemy. When the entire match depends on that final three-foot putt, you will discover just what we mean. Even the pros can succumb to a bout of nerves.

Next time you visit the practice green, try sinking in three-foot putts with your eyes closed. Closing your eyes makes you feel the putting stroke. Since you aren't looking at anything, you won't feel as nervous.

Reading the Green

In order to be a good putter, you must be able to read the putting green.

Reading the green is a combination of proper putting techniques including a good putting swing and knowing where to aim and target your ball. Before you take out your putter and swing, you need to read the green. In this section, we'll provide some guidelines on reading the green:

- **Slope Of The Green** – The slope of the green will affect both the speed and direction. There are only two angles to read. The first is the up-down angle. You see this angle from the side or from an angle perpendicular to the line of putt. You want to determine whether your ball is lying below or above the hole. If the ball is below, you need to hit harder and vice versa.

  The next angle is the left-right angle. You see this angle along the line of putt or behind the ball. Some golfers hold their putter at eye level for a better view.

  Angles become more complicated when more than one slope is involved.

- **Grass Length** – The simple formula is common sense. Grass causes resistance. Therefore, the longer the grass, the more resistance. This means the ball will roll slower.

- **Firmness** – Treat firmness as hardness. A hard surface has less resistance than a soft surface. Therefore, the firmer the green, the faster the roll. Warning: You aren't allowed to press your putter on the ground to test for firmness.

- **Moisture** – Moisture also causes resistance. More moisture means more resistance. Wet grass can really slow a ball down.

- **Direction Of Grass** – See which way the grass is pointing or the grain. Your ball will roll slower against the grain than along the grain.

- **Type Of Grass** – Your ball will travel faster on Bent grass than on Bermuda. You don't have to worry about grains with Bent grass.

- **Wind** – Just like in the air, wind also affects your ball on the ground. Your ball will roll faster with the wind and slower against the wind.

Observing the behavior of another golfer's ball will provide some idea of the green's characteristics. This is even more apparent if the golfer's line of putt is close to yours. However, it's not considered proper etiquette to stand in front or behind a golfer when he is putting.

Bear in mind that this reading only applies if your ball is more than 4 feet from the hole. If your ball is within 4 feet of the hole, you should forget about wind, grain or firmness. Unless the slope is really severe, you should even forget about the slope. Just aim for the back of the cup and firmly stroke the ball. At this distance, the momentum will send the ball into the cup before any of the above factors come into play.

Specialty Shots - Shot Making

How to Hit a Fade

Characteristics

Your ball starts straight and then curves slowly to the right.

Unlike the slice, the fade is a controllable shot which is helpful to know.

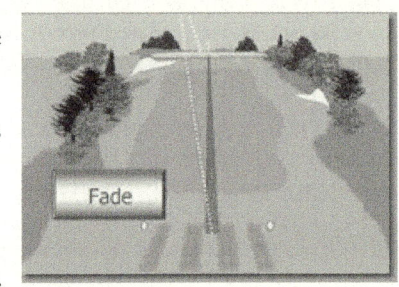

1. Set your clubface square to the ball.
2. Align your feet and shoulders to the left of the target – assume an open stance.
3. Pull your clubhead along your body alignment. It should go slightly to the outside of the target line. Your clubface should remain pointing to the target line.
4. Swing normally across your body line. This creates an out-to-in swing.
5. Concentrate on bringing the club back across the ball on the downswing.
6. Swinging a bit harder also encourages a fade.

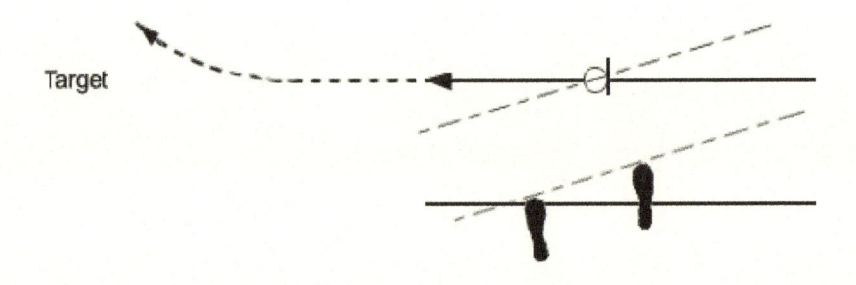

How to Hit a Draw

A study was conducted by Golf Digest to determine the distance traveled by the golf ball by two shots: the fade and the draw. Under similar conditions, the draw outdistanced the fade by 17 yards.

That's a lot of yardage!

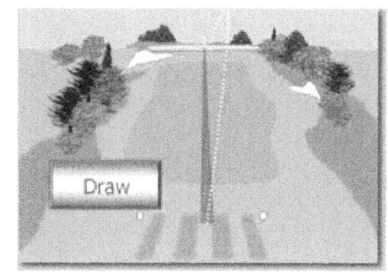

Characteristics

Your ball starts straight and then curves slowly to the left.

Unlike the hook, the draw is a controllable shot and very handy to know.

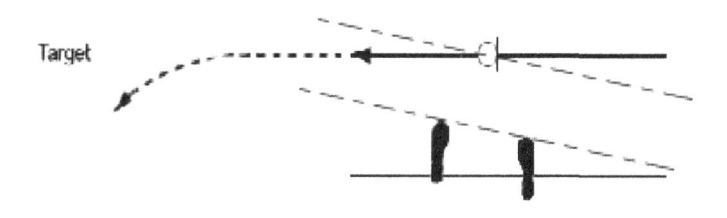

1. Stand more upright for a flatter swing.
2. Align your feet and shoulders to the right of the target –assume a closed stance.
3. Set your clubface square to the ball and facing the target line.
4. Pull your clubhead along your body alignment. It should go slightly to the inside of the target line. Your clubface should remain pointing to the target line.
5. Swing across your body line. This creates an in-to-out swing.
6. Let your right hand roll over your left hand through impact.

How to Hit a Knockdown Shot

As the name suggests, 'knockdown' means knocking the ball down *(B)* – not to the ground, but sending the ball on a lower trajectory than your normal flight *(A)*. The knockdown shot imparts less spin on to the ball.

To play a knockdown shot:

1. Adopt a narrower stance
2. Position the ball back in the stance
3. Choke down on the club
4. Make a steeper downswing
5. Limit the follow-through

When to play this shot:

- When you want to keep the trajectory of your ball lower than usual – especially in a windy condition
- When you want to have a better feel of the strength necessary to control the distance in between clubs
- When you want to decrease the amount of spin on the ball
- When you can't execute a normal backswing

How to Play to Low Shot

A low shot is not a knockdown shot, although it also flies low. The ball travels much farther than the knockdown show. It's a great shot to get your ball flying under those trees and on to the fairway.

To play a low shot:

1. Choose the right club. When the lie is clean, use a 5 or 6 iron. If the ball is in thick rough, use a 7 or 8 iron.
2. The ball position should be back toward your right foot.
3. Your hands should be in front of the ball to de-loft the club.
4. Keep your weight on your left leg.
5. Swing slower and flatter than usual. The slow speed helps to lessen the backspin that causes the ball to rise up.
6. Keep your hands low during the follow-through.

How to Play a Lob Shot

A lob shot is a high flying shot that lands on the green with little or no roll. It is used to send the ball over an obstacle such as a pond, tree or bunker on to the green. When you have very little green to work with and the lie is good enough, you can slide your club under the ball.

To play the lob you want to use a lob-wedge. This wedge has a loft of 60°.

To Play A Lob Shot:

1. Decide how far you want the ball to travel.
2. Open your clubface to add extra loft to the shot.
3. Angle your club 5 yards to the right of your target.
4. Angle your feet 5 yards to the left of your target.
5. Distribute weight evenly on both feet.
6. Bring the club back along the line of your feet.
7. Swing through the ball but don't allow the clubface to turn over.
8. Finish with the clubface open or pointing up to the sky.

Practice the lob shot on the driving range to determine how far the ball travels.

Tips & Warnings

- Practice with different swing speeds and angles of alignment.
- Keep your head down.
- A lob shot usually travel less than 30 yards.
- If a ball is sitting up in the rough, your club may slide under the ball and the ball will go nowhere.

Hit Down to Go Up

One of the paradoxes of golf is you have to hit down for the ball to go up.

Most beginners try to scoop the ball up with their clubhead when they want the ball to go up. By doing so, they dig up a chunk of earth instead of the ball.

This is called a 'fat shot'.

To contact the ball solidly, you must hit the ball first, then the ground. Your clubhead touches the ground just ahead of the ball.

Find a practice area with natural grass and push two tees into the ground about a foot apart. Place a ball on the line between the two tees. Your object is to hit the ball first and then divot the ground. Your divot mark should be in front of the line formed by the two tees – on the target side.

Remember to transfer your weight to your front foot before impact.

Playing in the Wind

The majority of golfers don't like wind. Wind upsets their normal rhythm, affects their judgment and even drives some golfers crazy.

Instead of joining the crowd, let the wind help you.

Here are a few things you should know when the wind blows:

First of all, you need some experience to gauge the strength of the wind. Knowing approximately how strong the wind is will help you decide what club to use. The standard rule is one club number for every 10 mph.

When playing in the wind, always remember: "Swing easy when it's breezy."

Headwind

A headwind is wind blowing towards your face. This is the hardest to play. You may tend to swing harder because you know the wind is going to slow down your ball. However, swinging harder makes it easier for you to make mistakes.

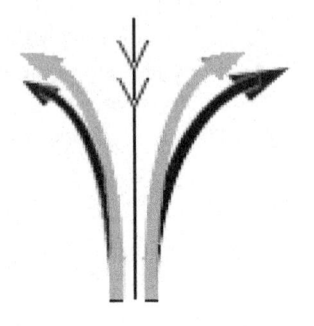

The headwind will amplify whatever mistakes you make as shown by the darker arrows in the diagram.

Swing easier. An easier swing imparts less spin. The wind amplifies the effect of the spin in a ball. So the less spin is imparted, the less chance the ball will stray off track. The wind will also magnify a slice and a fade. Therefore, you have to make allowance for it. A draw is less affected because it's on a lower.

This is one situation where you need to play the knockdown shot.
See Techniques – The Knockdown Shot.

Tailwind

A tailwind is a great ego booster. It makes you feel as if you're a pro. The wind will carry your ball farther and make it go straighter even if you mishit the ball as shown by the darker arrows.

For distance and carry, play the ball a little forward in your stance to hit it higher. Playing the ball back will make it easier to control.

The ball will roll longer in a tailwind.

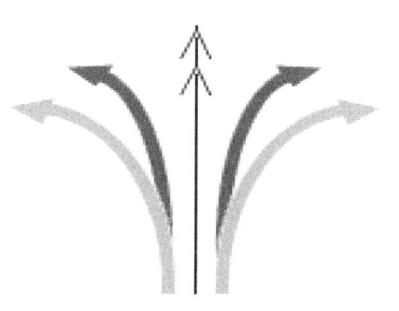

Crosswind

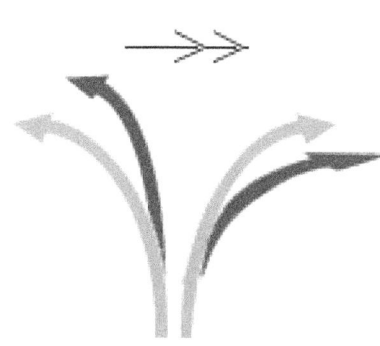

A crosswind is one that blows from left to right or right to left.

A crosswind that is blowing over 10 mph is going to affect a shot's flight, especially high, soft shots. It's better to play a knock-down with a 7-iron than to loft a 9-iron to the green.

For farther distances, you have two choices: go with the wind or against it.

Experience has shown that it's better to play against the wind. The canceling effect of the wind makes the end result more predictable.

With a light crosswind of less than 10 mph, play against the wind. For a left-to-right breeze, hit a draw into it. For a right-to-left breeze, hit a fade. Just aim straight at the target. The wind's direction will cancel your curve and make the ball go straight. Even if the wind's strength changes, your ball will be close to your target.

The same goes for winds of more than 10 mph. However, you need to aim the ball more to the left of the target for a strong left-to-right wind, and more to the right for a right-to-left wind.

You will know how far left or right you must aim through experience. To help you aim properly, find a secondary target and align your ball to it.

Solid contact is the primary object in any windy situation.

Learn to love the wind. It makes golf more exciting!

Troubleshooting

Diagnosing the Push Shot

Characteristics

Your ball starts to the right for a right-handed golfer and continues to fly straight along that line of flight. You will find your ball right of the target. If you look at the divot you make, it will also point to the right.

Below is a checklist of possible causes of the push shot. See which one correctly describes your fault and make the necessary adjustments:

Checklist

Grip: Not a factor here.

Ball position: Your ball is placed too far back in your stance. You hit the ball before your clubhead reaches the bottom of the swing.

Stance: Your stance is too wide.

Body alignment : Your feet, hips and shoulders are pointing too far to the right.

Posture: Your body weight is back on your heels instead of forward on the balls of your feet.

Swing:
- On your backswing, you're taking the club back too far inside. This will pull your club away from the target line.
- On your downswing, your club is swinging toward the right and your head is following that direction.
- You drop your head before you start your downswing.
- Your hips are sliding towards the target instead of turning.

Shock Tactics for Practice: The next time you visit a driving range, choose the rightmost bay. Try hitting balls to the left side of the range.

Diagnosing the Pull Shot

Characteristics

Your ball starts out flying left of the target and continues to fly along that line.

Below is a checklist of possible causes of the pull shot. See which one correctly describes your fault and make the necessary adjustments:

Checklist

Grip: Both your hands are twisted too far to your right making too strong a grip. This closes your clubface at impact.

Ball position: Your ball is too far forward in your stance.

Stance: Your stance is too narrow making the shoulders dominate the forward swing.

Body alignment : Your body alignment is pointing too far left.

Posture: Not enough knee flex.

Swing:
- You push your club towards the outside of the target line on your backswing.
- Your club is over your head at the top of your backswing when it should be over your shoulder.
- You are pushing your arms away from your body during the transition.
- You move your head toward the target during your downswing.

Shock Tactics for Practice: Open your clubface during backswing and close it after you hit the shot.

Diagnosing the Slice

Characteristics

Your ball starts to the left of the target and half way it starts to turn right until it finishes well right of the target.

Below is a checklist of possible causes of the slice. See which one correctly describes your fault and make the necessary adjustments:

Checklist

Grip: Your left hand is turned too far to the left resulting in a weak grip. This causes your club to become open at impact.

Ball position: You position the ball to far forward.

Stance: Your stance is too narrow which causes instability.

Body alignment: Your body alignment is pointing too far left of the target. This will cause an "out-to-in" swing.

Posture: You are standing too far from the ball.

Swing:
- You are taking the clubhead too far to the outside on your backswing
- Your shoulder is going out instead of down, resulting in your arms being pushed away from you as you swing down. This causes an out-to-in swing
- Your wrist is blocking your club from turning over.
- You are relying too much on your arms instead of your hips.

Shock Tactics for Practice: Find a side hill lie and place balls above your feet. Practice hitting on this lie which will help you swing along the correct line.

Diagnosing the Unwanted Fade

The fade is a good technique to have and can prove useful when the situation warrants. However, some golfers tend to hit a fade all the time. This is a problem because a fade produces less distance.

If you consistently hit a fade, look at the following checklist to determine the cause:

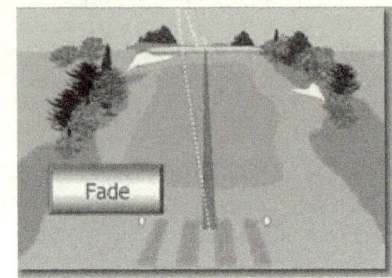

Checklist

Grip: Both your hands are twisted too far to your right making too strong a grip. This closes your clubface at impact.

Ball position: Your ball is too far forward in your stance.

Stance: Your stance is too narrow making the shoulders dominate the forward swing.

Body alignment : Your body alignment is pointing too far left.

Posture: Not enough knee flex.

Swing:
- You push your club towards the outside of the target line on your backswing.
- Your club is over your head at the top of your backswing when it should be over your shoulder.
- You are pushing your arms away from your body during the transition.
- You move your head toward the target during your downswing.

Shock Tactics for Practice: Open your clubface during backswing and close it after you hit the shot.

Diagnosing & Curing the Hook

Characteristics

Your ball starts to the right of the target, curves to the left and finishes to the left of the target. A hook devastates golfers more than any other shot.

Below is a checklist of possible causes. Find your fault and make the necessary adjustments:

Checklist

Grip: Your left hand is turned too far to the right.

The "V" formed by your thumb and forefinger should point between your right shoulder and right ear, not outside your shoulder.
You shouldn't see more than 2 knuckles on your left hand.

Ball position: Your ball may be too far back in your stance.

Stance: Your stance may be too wide.

Body alignment: Your shoulders and feet are aligned too far right of the target.

Swing: It's not easy to hook a ball unless you're doing something drastic:

- You are taking the club back too far inside during your backswing. Look at your club at the end of your backswing. Your shaft should be over your shoulder, not behind it.
- You begin your downswing by a counter-clockwise action, closing the clubface. This is the most probable cause for most golfers.
  On your backswing the turning of your shoulders should 'open' your clubface, not the twisting of your hands.
- During the downswing, your shoulder is lowering too much, accompanied with a sliding of your hips toward the target. You should start your downswing by shifting your weight to your left foot and turning your body.
- You are muscling the swing. Make sure your hands and arms are relaxed.
- You are directing the club too much to the right at impact. Try to keep the club moving at the target line.

Shock Tactics for Practice: Try to keep the clubface open all the way.

Topping the Ball

Topping the ball occurs when your clubhead contacts the ball above its equator.

What are the causes?

1. During set-up, your body is tilted. When you are about to hit the ball, your body rises. This causes the clubhead to rise up as well which results in topping.

2. During set-up, your arms are straight. When you are about to hit the ball, your arms are bent. This shortens the swing arc and contacts the ball higher up.

Is there a cure? Yes. A simple one.

First ask yourself the following question. What makes you raise your body or bend your arms? Most times it's because you want to crush the ball. You're trying to hit the ball too hard.

The cure is to relax. Don't swing so hard. Never swing at more than 80% of your full strength.

Casting

Have you ever wondered some skinny ladies can hit the ball farther than you? Her movements seem so smooth and effortless, yet her drive travels 10 yards farther than yours.

You don't have to be a big to hit a long ball. The trick is the wrist snap that gives the extra oomph to your swing. Timing is very important.

Many short hitters do not fully hinge their wrists. More short hitters snap their wrists too early on the downswing. This is called casting, and it's similar to a fisherman casting his rod. The result of casting is a loss of clubhead speed. You can make solid contact, but your ball will lack the extra kick to propel it farther.

For that extra kick, you must delay your wrist snap until the very last moment.

The answer is your right hand. Your right hand must hinge at, or just before, the top of your backswing. As you swing down, your hand must remain hinged until the last moment.

Before we proceed further, we need to distinguish between the two wrist actions.

Cock forward   Cock backward

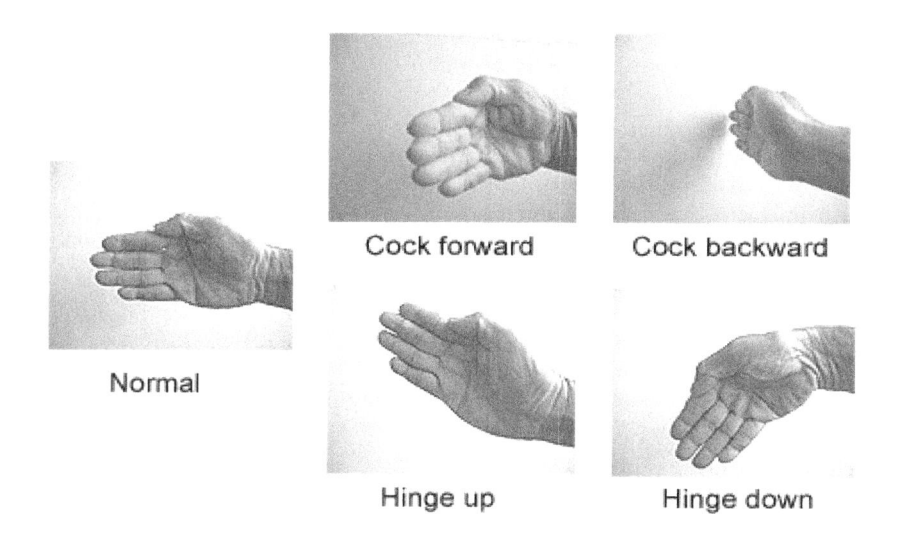

Normal

Hinge up   Hinge down

Cocking is the bending of the hand backward or forward.

Hinging is the bending of the hand upward or downward. In a golf swing, the hinging action sets the club, not the cocking action.

When you swing your club to the top of your backswing, your wrist is hinged. During the downswing, as your hands drop to your hip level, your wrists must remain hinged. This is where most golfers straighten their wrists. The angle between your club shaft and your arm should remain perpendicular. The butt of your club should be pointing toward the target.

Visualize pulling the rope of a church-bell downward.

The farther you can keep this angle, the closer to impact is your release. Try doing this without a ball. Once you can hit your target on the ground consistently, place a ball there. You'll be able to see how lively the ball will travel.

Course Management

How to Handle Awkward Lies

Hills give the golf course a natural beauty. They also provide golfers with natural challenges to prove their mettle. The inclinations of a hill can pose problems. This is what can end up separating the men from the boys during a game.

For the big hitter, the problem is compounded because any error is magnified. Here are some scenarios you're likely to encounter on a hilly course:

Downhill - Ball Below Your Feet

This is a difficult lie. The ball will tend to go right so you can't swing aggressively.

Woods are out for this hole, unless you have a modern iron-wood with a high lofts. For irons, a 3-iron is the maximum club you can play.

Because of the nature of the lie, you may lose your balance if too much body action is involved. This is one area where you will have to play using arm-swing only. Therefore, take an extra club or two whenever possible.

Since the ball tends to fly right, you may expect a slice. Consequently, you aim left of the target. Play the ball forward in your stance, toward your left heel. Do NOT swing hard. Muscling of the ball will cause you to lose balance and mishit the ball.

Downhill - Ball Above Your Feet

There is a tendency for the ball to go left. However, you may end up hitting a thin shot and send the ball to the right. The nature of this lie encourages your body to slide downhill on the downswing.

Adopt a wider stance to reduce this slide. Play the ball toward the back and aim slightly to the right.

If you are using fairway woods, expect the ball to run a long way. If the slope is severe, use less club.

Uphill - Ball Below Your Feet

As long as the ball is below your feet, there's a tendency for your body to slide down. In order not to slide, you need to inhibit your body movement and rely on your arm swing only. However, you can be more aggressive in an uphill lie.

Slopes cancel each other out and you don't have to adjust for the shot going left or right. Just aim for a straight shot. Play the ball farther back in your stance to encourage a steeper contact.

Uphill – Ball Above Your Feet

This ball is going left. Of the four lies, this is the easiest one to handle.

The uphill adds loft and encourages the ball to go high. Take one more club to counteract the loft and aim right. This will counteract the left-favored direction of the slope.

The slope may also make you fall back and loop the club around. Take the club straight back and swing along your body line. Drive through the ball with your body to avoid pulling it.

Red Flag

The red flag on the green means the hole is located at the front end of the green. For most golfers, the red flag spells trouble.

The reason is there's very little green to work with in front of the flag. Unlike a professional golfer, a high-handicapper usually can't produce enough backspin to make the ball move backwards. Thus, he has to resort to pitching or chipping the ball on the ground before the green.

Getting the ball close to the pin will depend a lot on the first bounce. This bounce will depend on where the ball lands.

Below are a few areas to watch:

Slopes

Very few greens are completely flat. You will see slopes leading to the green itself. The contour of the slope is important. If the slope is uphill, you know your ball will roll slower and stop quicker. Downhill is even trickier. You don't want to send the ball rolling past the hole for a three-putt. A slope to the right will send the ball to the right and vice versa.

High or Low Greens

If the green is located above you, your ball will land on a lower angle and roll faster. To stop it, you should play a high flop that drops down on a steep angle.

On the other hand, a green below you will deaden the momentum of the ball because of the higher angle of entry. To make sure your ball reaches the green, you may have to play a low running shot.

Grain

Grain is the direction the grass on the green is growing. It can be difficult to see from afar. Of course, you can always walk right up to the green to see the grain when you are chipping from less than 20 yards. If you see a shiny surface, you are looking at the back of grass blades that are pointing away from you. This means your ball will roll faster.

You can also determine the direction of the grain by the presence of water near the green. Grain will generally be pointing towards the water.

How to Play the Par 3

Don't mess around with a Par 3.

Nearly all golfers can reach this hole with one shot. Very few Par 3 holes exceed 180 yards. Surely you have a club that will reach that distance. Making a bogey is bad and a double bogey is a sin.

Play your shot carefully when facing a Par 3. Nine out of ten golfers will shoot short of the pin. Four out of ten will not reach the green altogether. So, take enough club to reach the flag. If the flag is 150 yards and your best shot for that yardage is a 6-iron, use a 5-iron.

Why?

How many times have you played your best shot?

Consider your starting tee. The distance should be shown on the board next to the tee box. Keep in mind that the distance is from middle of the tee to the middle of the green, not to the hole.

Also check out the flag position. You are shooting for the flag in a Par-3, not just the green. Look at the color of the flag. Red means in front. White means in the middle, and blue at the back. Depending on the size of the green, blue and red can mean one more club.

As you see the flag observe the wind direction. Sometimes the wind direction at the tee box is different at the green. Wind at the green plays a greater importance than wind at the tee box.

Is the green higher than you?

If so, your ball will roll more as a result of a low angle of entry. If the green is lower, your ball will come to a faster stop.

Lastly, always use a tee. Tee the ball low so you can take a divot and create some backspin on the ball to let it stop faster.

Cold Weather Play

Ice, snow and chilling winds. All of these elements are just around the corner. It's time to put away your golf set and stay indoors. After Labor Day, the only hole golfers are interested in is the 19th.

Not for you. For a beginner, fall is the best time to play. Mother Nature is at her most splendid moment. Trees turn golden, the heat wave is gone, golf courses are not crowded, no more serious tournaments and the hustlers are gone. It's time to enjoy the scenery and play some relaxing golf.

You'll be surprised at how much better you play.

Since courses are relatively empty, you will probably be able to play alone.
This is the best opportunity for you to improve your short game skills. You know that you depend heavily on this part of the game. Now is the best time to hone these skills. Leave the big sticks in your closet.

Forget about taking a scorecard. Play target golf. Right from the tee-off, treat the fairway as a part of the green. Look for a particular spot and see if you can pitch your ball there. You can do this all the way to the green. Purposely pitch your ball into a bunker.

This is also the time for you to try out some variations. Instead of playing your usual high pitch on to the green, try the pitch and run. This is the time to add more skills to your arsenal. What you previously practiced on the driving range can be practiced right here on the course.

By the end of the round, you should find yourself getting nearer to your targets. You may even hit some directly!

On the green, you can polish your putting skills. No one will rush you. You can take your time reading the line. You can even move to another part of the green, drop a ball and then play. It will be like having nine different practice greens to practice. Playing nine holes is sufficient since you will spend longer at each hole.

You'll also have a great chance to practice in windy conditions. Use this opportunity to hone your wind playing skills.

You'll be wearing more clothing to keep your body warm in the open. This clothing can be a hindrance to your normal summer swing. If you insist on using that swing with all the clothing, your timing will suffer and you'll miss the sweet spot. The proper technique for the cold is to use a shorter backswing.

With the short backswing, your downswing will also be smooth and short. Your aim is to try and make solid contact. This technique applies to both your irons and your woods. The idea is to keep everything under control. When playing the irons, use a longer club to achieve the distance you normally get in summer.

Making a shorter swing doesn't mean swinging abruptly. Swing smooth and easy. Just take your backswing smoothly and stop when you feel the extra attire is in the way. That's the distance for your backswing. Let the word 'comfortable' be the guide to your play.

If you try swinging the way you did in summer with all your extra clothing, you'll create a bad swing. This can carry over and ruin your game when hot weather returns and all the extra clothing is gone.

On the other hand, keeping your swing smooth and short during winter will not hamper your game later on. Once summer arrives, your longer swing will come back naturally without all your cumbersome attire. In fact, your swing may even be smoother and more relaxed. This smooth and relaxed swing may be just what you need to propel that ball farther and more under control.

If you think you can use your normal swing by wearing less clothing, forget it. You need to be comfortably warm. If you develop a chill, your game will suffer. Long johns and corduroy slacks will be sufficient. For your upper body, wear several layers of lighter clothing instead of one thick garment. Wear a loose-fitting polyester windbreaker as your outer shell. Also use a scarf around your neck. Too warm is better than too cold. Top it off with a stocking cap. In extra cold weather, wear a ski band under your stocking cap to protect your ears. Make sure you also take a golf visor.

You need to be well equipped for the cold wind. Wear extra layers. Ordinary sweaters won't protect you adequately. Wear a nylon-type jacket as the top layer and wear long johns. It won't be any fun if the chill gets you. This is one case where more is better. You can always remove some clothing, but you can't add clothing you don't have.

Unfortunately, fall is followed by winter. But winter isn't barrier if weather permits. You need to make some adjustments for the winter.

1. Make sure your grips are in good condition, especially when wet. Clean your grips with a stiff brush and detergent. Swarfega is great for cleaning grips.

2. Make sure you wear or bring good waterproofs. Your shoes should also be waterproof. Wear all-weather gloves. You should also carry winter mitts, a nylon slip-on, a spare towel and a warm stocking cap.

Rough Play

As a beginner, you'll probably find your ball in the rough more often than on the fairway. Many golfers want to try for the green no matter what. Most of the time, they find themselves in worse trouble. You have to reconsider your game plan. You need to know how fast you can swing and the kind of a lie a ball is situated.

Don't be influenced by what you see on TV. The pros can make every rough shot look easy. They're not. The pros can generate tremendous swing speed to fly the ball out toward the green. If you can't swing fast enough, you'll require a more lofted club to get the ball out of the rough – a 9-iron or a pitching wedge. These clubs won't give you distance.

Let's take a look at the two kinds of lies:

Deep Lie

A deep lie is one where the ball is well inside the grass. When confronted with this situation, forget about getting the ball to travel far. Bringing the ball out on to the fairway should be your only goal.

Use the 9-iron or pitching wedge. Square the ball with the clubface. Your weight should be toward your left leg. Position the ball a little further back. This gives you a steeper entry angle.

To gain more control, hold the club further down the shaft. Use a three-quarter swing. Don't try to scoop the ball up like most beginners. Strike down aggressively. Keep a firm hold of the club to prevent the clubface from turning. You should also aim slightly to the right of the target because the grass will grab your heel and turn it left.

You don't have to swing hard. Use a smooth blow and keep your left hand moving down. Follow through as long as you can. Don't worry about that the grass may impede your club and ruin your follow-through. A good crisp chop will place the ball safely on to the fairway. Be sure you keep your eyes focused on the ball. Many beginners are so anxious to see where their ball is heading, they look up prematurely and mishit.

The Flier Lie

A flier lie is when the ball sits on top of the grass as if it's being teed up for you. As the name implies, the ball tends to travel farther than usual.

Consider yourself lucky to find such a lie, but don't get carried away. It may be trickier than you think. You have to hit this ball with a sweeping motion similar to the tee-off. This will cause the ball to travel farther.

You need to judge the distance cautiously. Not only will the ball travel farther, the blades of grass will get in between your ball and your clubface. This will cause your ball to jump off the clubface and result in less backspin on the ball. You should use one or two clubs less than usual.

This ball will reach the green and possibly beyond. Don't aim for the flag if it's located at a corner. Play into the middle of the green. Use a normal three-quarter swing. You may be tempted to swing if you take a club less.

Regardless of whether your ball is lying deep or sitting up, you should check if there is trouble ahead. You don't want to go from the frying pan into the fire. Play smart if there is a bunker or water ahead. Hit to a spot where you can make a good chip.

The 70 Per Cent Trick

You crack a huge swing at the ball on a long par-5 and watch it sailing out of bounds. You decide to play the next shot more conservatively and make a half swing. Though your ball remains in play, you don't like what you see. What's the matter? You swing hard and the ball goes haywire. You swing soft and the ball also goes haywire. How else can you swing?

You have to find your comfort zone. If anything beyond three-quarters of your full swing is uncontrollable, then you should stay below that limit. Similarly, if you cannot swing slower than 60%, don't go slower than that. Of course, we are talking about the full swing, and not chipping or pitching.

Make sure you are fully warmed up before this exercise. Once your muscles are loose and ready, make 10 full swings with your driver. Swing as hard as you possibly can without stopping. By the time you finish all ten swings, you will probably be breathless. Now you are ready.

Tee a ball up. Swing again but use only 70% of your previous swing. Since you are well within your comfort zone, you should be able to control this swing. You may be surprised to see how far the ball flies.

You may think you are using only 70%. Actually the percentage is probably closer to 85%. Your previous 10 hard swings are more than your full swing; they may be 120%. 70% of that will bring it to about 85% of your normal full swing. So you are really swinging at 85%.

Since you are actually swinging at 70% and feeling comfortable, your ball is under better control.

Do you do this all the time? Not necessarily. As you proceed into the round, you may find your pace and tempo affected by surrounding situations. You may have to wait a long time for the group in front to move on. The sun may be getting hotter. You might get tired. All of these factors can upset your rhythm. You will start swinging harder and harder. This is the time you should use your hard practice swings. Relax and hit that ball 70%.

Play to your strengths. If you want to see flustered, relax, keep the ball on the fairway and watch in delightful bemusement as your male counterpart flails his way from one side of the fairway rough to the next muscling his way around the course.

Getting More Distance
One reason women don't get much distance is a lack of strength in their upper bodies, arms and wrists. A daily program of exercise designed to strengthen the hands, arms, wrists, legs, chest, and back will definitely help increase your driving distance however this is awfully tiring.

You don't need strength to get distance but you do need to be able to swing the club effectively. Women lose distance through too many power-leaks in their set-up and swing.

Set-up: Bend from the hips
Many women lose power right from their set-up. Generally, women stand far too straight at address with too much weight on their toes. This provides them with poor balance, which impedes a proper weight shift and body turn. When this happens you can't generate enough clubhead speed (what really gets you distance - not strength) and hit the ball solidly. Knees should be flexed. Bend from the hips - not the waist. Weight is over the middle of your feet. This posture will allow your arms to hang tension-free and whip the club into impact position at maximum speed.

Backswing: Make a strong shoulder turn
The poor address position above usually leads to tilting the body rather than turning the body on the backswing. This results in a very poor weight shift and no ability to generate any clubhead speed at all.

To get power into your backswing with control, only take a three-quarter length backswing but make a full shoulder turn. You should feel as if you are pivoting around your spine with your left shoulder ending up under your chin.

Downswing: Clear your hips
Due to the faulty set-up, and loose upright backswing, the woman player swings down so steeply that the resulting shot is a weak pop-up.
Good balance at address, a full wrist cock and a full shoulder turn will put you in good position at the top of your backswing. from here let your shoulders unwind and hips clear to the left of the target. The result will be an effortless downswing - and longer and straighter shots.

Fitness Tips for Lady Golfers

IMPORTANT: Use these exercises we recommend at your own risk. It is recommended that, before beginning any exercise program, individuals seek advice from their physician or a certified exercise professional. The exercises and stretches listed on this web site should be done slowly and carefully. If you feel pain or discomfort STOP IMMEDIATELY!

Stretching: All Natural Golf Training Aide

You can use golf training aides no matter how high your skill level is. Whether you're a scratch player or a scrappy beginner, you can always stand to improve your game. After all, you want to be able to beat your friends consistently and win those bets on who can drive the farthest, who can make that tough double-break putt, and who can match up hole to hole.

The best way to ensure total domination of the other players in your group is to train and practice. Buy those buckets of golf balls at the driving range. Tinker around the putting green shot after shot. Practice your short game in your backyard during those free moments between hotdogs on the grill. And don't forget to stretch!

That's right. Golf training aides and practice is not all about perfecting your swing or adjusting your grip. Part of the process means fine-tuning your body to perform at its peak for all eighteen holes. There is no better way to fine-tune your muscles and joints before and after a round than stretching.

First off, stretching before the first tee helps to minimize your risk of injury. You can't compete with your buddies if you have a strained rotator cuff. What's more, stretching offers concrete benefits like increased flexibility, increased stamina, and better performance.

For those of you who never played much sports in school, or played so long ago that they forget their pre-game calisthenics, here are a couple stretching golf training aides to get you started. First, don't forget to warm up a bit before stretching. This could mean a brisk walk to the clubhouse or around the club. Swing your club a few times. Carry your bag to the driving range.

Once you're warmed up, get to stretching. Whatever stretch you do, don't bounce or move fast. Stretch out slowly and smoothly, holding at the farthest point you can stretch. Never extend yourself to the point it hurts. Hold each stretch for at least 30 seconds, and repeat twice only if necessary.

Golf Resistance Training

Golf resistance training is the key to improving your score, enjoying the game more, and feeling better, too. No matter your age, resistance training can help you get into shape and stave off disease.

For golfers, resistance training, or strength training as it's also known, can help add power to their swing, boost endurance for making it through all 18 holes, and loosen muscles to prevent injury. Resistance training involves lifting weights or working out on machines at a gym. You can
also, though, do resistance training at home using everyday items around your home.

To start, first and foremost talk with doctor. Resistance training should be considered strong "medicine," if only because you could hurt yourself if you don't know what you're doing or aren't sure how hard you should be working out. Once you're doctor gives you the green light, you have another important hurdle to cross. Should you or shouldn't you join a gym? This question is actually simply solved with a little effort. Locate the gyms in your area and visit each one. Most gyms will give you a free tour, or even a free week's worth of workouts. So take advantage of these offers to check out the clientele and determine if you will be comfortable and satisfied with the equipment.

If your decide that you don't feel comfortable at a gym, or if you don't want to foot the bill for one, you can do your golf resistance training at home. When you first start out, you may not even need to buy any dumbbells or other equipment.

For instance, one great exercise for your legs involves just squatting down. You can lean against a ball for support or do it in the middle of the room for a harder workout. Start by placing your hands on your hips. Then bend your knees while keeping your back straight. Lower down as far as comfortable, or until your thighs are 90 degrees to the floor. Push up.

Another great golf resistance training exercise for your legs involves sitting in a chair. Scoot the front of the seat, keeping your back straight. With one foot planted on the floor, straighten your other leg until it is parallel to the ground. Repeat with the other leg.

How to Prevent Golf Injuries

Many people consider golf a low-level physical activity without the possibility of injury ever happening to them. But, there is a potential risk of suffering serious injuries to the elbow, spine, knee, hip or wrist.
Before hitting the links, golfers can take some preventive measures to protect themselves against injury.

Golfer's elbow - Leading the list of injuries is golfer's elbow, and one of the best ways to avoid elbow problems is to strengthen the forearm muscles and slow the swing so that there will be less shock in the arm when the ball is hit by the golfer.
To avoid golfer's elbow, the American Academy of Orthopaedic Surgeons suggests these simple exercises to help build up your forearm muscles.

- **Squeeze a tennis ball** - Squeezing a tennis ball for five minutes at a time is a simple, effective exercise that will strengthen your forearm muscles.

- **Wrist curls** - Use a lightweight dumbbell. Lower the weight to the end of your fingers, then curl the weight back into your palm, followed by curling up your wrist to lift the weight an inch or two higher. Perform 10 repetitions with one arm, then repeat with the other arm.

- **Reverse wrist curls** - Use a lightweight dumbbell. Place your hands in front of you, palm side down. Using your wrist, lift the weight up and down. Hold the arm that you are exercising above your elbow with your other hand in order to limit the motion to your forearm. Perform 10 repetitions with one arm, then repeat with the other arm.

Low back pain - Another common complaint among golfers, low back pain, can be caused by a poor swing. The rotational stresses of the golf swing can place considerable pressure on the spine and muscles. Also poor flexibility and muscle strength can cause minor strains in the back that can easily become severe injuries.
Here are some simple exercises to help strengthen lower back muscles and prevent injuries.

- **Pull-downs** - Firmly tie the ends of rubber tubing. Place it around an object that is shoulder height (like a door hinge). Standing with your arms straight out in front of you, grasp the tubing and slowly pull it toward your chest. Release slowly. Perform three sets of 10 repetitions, at least three times a week.

- **Rowing** - With the rubber tubing still around the door hinge, kneel and hold the tubing over your head. Pull down slowly toward your chest, bending your elbows as you lower your arms. Raise the tubing slowly over your head. Perform three sets of 10 repetitions, at least three times a week.

But perhaps, one of the best ways for golfers to stretch their muscles and avoid injury could be considered old-fashioned-before your round of golf, engage in some simple stretching exercises, and then get a bucket of balls and hit a few golf balls on the driving range. It not only will help your game, but will make you healthier in the long run.

A Lot of you ladies have been asking "Please tell me what exercise to do to get rid of those love handles on my hips and sides of my stomach that hang over the sides of my pants."

The belief that you can somehow spot reduce is a persistent misunderstanding among exercisers. If you could spot reduce, then doing thousands of sit-ups would melt away your spare tire. But as many have found out the hard way, this simply won't work. Specific exercises will not result in loss of body fat from specific areas. Period.

"Love Handles" are just genetically determined places on an individual's body where excess fat tends to be stored. Every individual is different and your problem areas may be different from mine. Respect the fact that your metabolism is different from everyone else's, and as unique as your fingerprint. The only way to lose fat deposited on any area of the body is to reduce the overall level of fat storage. Sensible eating habits designed to reduce calorie intake and regular exercise designed to burn off excess calories will help reduce overall body-fat stores.

Try to maintain a consistent schedule that includes 30-45 minutes of aerobic exercise 3-4 times a week or more. In addition, doing a total-body strength-training routine twice a week will increase your lean body composition, which will help you burn more calories even when you're at rest. This in turn will further enable you to reduce your overall fat stores, including those love handles, saddlebags, etc. As for diet, eat five or six small, low-fat meals a day to keep your blood sugar steady and your metabolism stoked and to prevent cravings and pig-outs (more on that below).

Remember doing hundreds of crunches, sit-ups and so forth will not reduce the fat stored in the abdominal region. It will, however, help tone the muscles in that area and help burn calories. You'll achieve better results by doing aerobic exercise and a total body, strength-training routine, targeting your middle with strength-training exercises and following the eating tips described below. I also highly recommend including Yoga exercises in your workout routine, so much so that I included a whole chapter on Yoga for female Golfers further down. This comes from own experience, and I cannot overemphasize the benefits it will bring to your game.

To help to get a handle on those love handles try these exercises:

You can improve the overall appearance of your waist by spot TRAINING to tone the muscles underneath the fat deposits. Doing 2-5 abdominal exercises twice a week will adequately train those

Twist crunch: This exercise works your *rectus abdominis* as well as your internal and external *obliques*, two muscle groups that wrap around your waist. Exhale through your mouth and curl your head, neck, and shoulders up and towards the left. Hold at the top of the movement, then lower to the start. Twist to the right on the next rep, and continue alternating until you complete the set. Note: Don't just twist your elbows from side to side. Really concentrate on twisting from your muscles so they become visible as you lose total body fat. Do 8-15 repetitions per set; move slowly and deliberately so you really feel every rep.

Basic crunch: Works the *rectus abdominis*, the wide flat muscle that runs from your breastbone to the top of your pelvis. Lie on the floor with your feet hip-width apart. Cradle your head in your hands without lacing your fingers together and with your elbows rounded slightly inward. Tilt your chin a small way towards your chest and pull your abdominal muscles in. Exhale through your mouth as you curl your head, neck, and shoulders up off the floor. Hold at the top of the movement for a moment, then inhale as you slowly lower down.

Anchoring: This exercise uses all of your abdominal muscles, including the deep, underlying *transverse abdominis*. Your lower back also gets a workout. Lie on your back with your left foot on the floor. Lift up your right leg and bend your knee so that your thigh is perpendicular to the floor and directly in line with your hip; flex your heel. Raise your arms up over your chest and clasp your fingers together. Slowly lower your heel and your arms towards the floor. As you do so, concentrate on keeping your abs pulled inward, and don't allow your lower back to pop up off the floor. This becomes harder the closer your heel and hands move towards the floor. When your heel has almost touched the floor, slowly return your arms and leg to the start. Repeat this exercise four times with your right leg, then four times with your left.

Weight Tips

Here are a few tips to help you watch your weight.

Sandwiches are often the lunch of choice during the work day, five days a week, 52 weeks a year. If you maintain the same diet and exercise schedule but eat your lunchtime sandwich without a tablespoon of mayonnaise, what could you expect to weigh a year from today? The answer is seven pounds less. One tablespoon of mayo contains 100 calories. So if you eat a sandwich every day, you consume an extra 500 calories per week. Over a year, that adds up to seven pounds.

Did you know that the color of the tablecloth you are eating off of can determine how much you eat?

What color tablecloth discourages you from eating? Dark green is a good choice under your plate and on top of it. Research shows colors can affect how you eat. "Color influences the process of eating much more in the overweight than the underweight," says Maria Simonson, director of the Health, Weight and Stress Program at Johns Hopkins Medical Institutions. Shades of dark green, dark blue and coffee-colored brown can help suppress your appetite. Orange, yellow and red tend to stimulate appetite and encourage overeating -- that's why many fast food restaurants decorate with them

What is the best time of day to exercise?

The crack of dawn is the best time to exercise is when you're most likely to follow through and actually do it. Generally speaking, this tends to be first thing in the morning. As the day grinds on, things tend to crop up and upset your schedule. Whether it's a long meeting, a surprise project due the next morning or a minicrisis at the daycare center, the slightest addition to your daily schedule can push exercise to the bottom of your priority list. Morning exercise, however, is almost impossible to excuse yourself from. And research suggests that a.m. exercisers are more likely to stick with it. So lay out your sneakers and set the alarm clock.

You're hosting a dinner party for your weight-conscious friends, so you're concerned about serving a healthy meal. Which menu is best for you and your guests?

A. A smorgasbord of low-fat foods, served buffet style

B. A low-fat casserole with grains, protein and vegetables.

C. The all-American four course meal: protein, starch, vegetable and dessert, all low in fat.

D. A classic seven-course meal, featuring dainty portions of crunchy, salty, spicy and sweet foods, all low in fat.

A low-fat casserole with grains, protein and vegetables. Faced with a wide array of tempting choices, most people can't resist sampling everything on the menu. Trouble is, "just a taste" of several different dishes usually adds up to more calories than you bargained for. Besides cutting down on cleanup, a one-dish meal adds up to easier portion control.

Eating to loose Weight

No weight loss program is complete without a exercise program, however it must go hand and hand with a change in eating habits. Even a moderate exercise plan in conjunction with following these basic rules should help you get to your goals!
The amount of fat you eat is probably less important than the kind of fat you eat. The worst are fried foods, margarine and foods that contain hydrogenated or partially hydrogenated oils. The best are the omega-3's found in fish and flaxseed oil.
Ninety percent of what you eat should be food that could have been plucked from a tree, gathered from the ground, hunted or caught.
Eat protein at every meal and drink at least eight or more large glasses of pure water a day. Every day. Eliminate wheat- and flour-based products for the time being. That definitely includes bread and pasta. Stop using vegetable oils such as sunflower, safflower and corn. The supermarket kind is highly refined, and it oxidizes easily when heated, contributing to arterial plaque.
If possible, fruit should be eaten alone. Eating fruit should not be unlimited: two a day, and only the lower-sugar, high-fiber variety such as berries, apples, pears, and plums. Because of the high sugar content Bananas are not good choices.
Reduce dairy, especially cow's milk. Exceptions: reasonable amounts of cheese and occasional portions of yogurt, but not the fat-free kind (it contains way too much sugar).
Only have one portion of starch a day, and try not to eat that portion during your evening meal. Best choices are oatmeal, sweet potatoes and beans.
Despite what the "studies" say, you lose no health benefits by giving up alcohol. There is nothing essential in alcohol that you can't get in fruits and vegetables.
No one is going to do this perfectly, but 90% is obtainable, and you will still get results!

Golf and Pregnancy

Golf can be started during pregnancy, even by those not currently participating in an exercise program.
Guidelines for Exercise During Pregnancy
Exercise programs should take into consideration your individual medical and exercise history. Consult with your physician before beginning or continuing an exercise program to see if you have any conditions which might restrict your physical activity during pregnancy.
STOP exercising and consult your physician if you experience any of the following symptoms during exercise:

- bleeding

- cramping

- faintness

- elevated blood pressure
- dizziness
- severe joint pain

Pregnant women should NOT exercise to exhaustion--stop when you are fatigued.
Exercise regularly and consistently. You should exercise at least three times per week. If you exercise more frequently, alternate hard and easy workouts. Drink plenty of fluids, especially water, before and after exercise to avoid becoming dehydrated. If your exercise session is longer than 15 minutes, interrupt your workout to drink additional liquids. Drink even if you are not thirsty, as thirst lags behind the body's need for fluids. A general guideline for exercise during pregnancy--consider your pre-pregnancy fitness and activity level. Most physically fit women can continue most activities at or slightly below levels prior to pregnancy. Do not try to exceed pre-pregnancy levels.
Other activities that can be started during pregnancy, even by those not currently participating in an exercise program are:

- low impact aerobics
- cycling/stationary biking
- rowing machine
- stairmaster /stair climbing
- swimming
- walking
- water aerobics

Tips for Stamina

Tips for stamina and concentration on the course:

1. Drink lots of water with electrolytes to hydrate your muscles and your brain.
2. Snacks for long term stamina (18 holes): apples, grapes, nuts, and popcorn.
3. Snacks for a quick energy burst: banana, raisins, carrots, and bagel.
4. If you are prone to temper outbursts, try munching on sunflower seeds, and carrots or have chicken or salmon for lunch. Their nutrients help calm nerves.
5. Back pain sufferers should avoid foods that contain high levels of uric acid, such as red meats, pasteurized dairy products and caffeine.
6. Stretching prior to play, can prevent tight muscles which can result in a limp or a crook in your neck and reduced performance.

7. If traveling to high altitude golf resort destinations, reduce your intake of high fat and high protein foods. These contribute to altitude sickness and lengthen your adjustment to low oxygen levels.

8. Women suffering from PMS can eat more chocolate, turkey, meat, wheat germ and ricotta cheese. These contain phenylalanine, a neuropepetide that supports specific mood regulating neurotransmitters in the brain.

9. Migraines may be lessened by eating: pickled products, bananas, prunes, raisins, cheese, beer and wine. They contain an amino acid that affects blood vessels.

10. Women with menopausal hot flashes should avoid trigger foods such as tobacco, caffeine, spicy foods and sugar which elevate adrenaline levels that contribute to the hot flash.

Improve your Golf with Yoga for Golfers

Why Yoga for Golfers?

Yoga is often seen just as another form of physical exercise, but that's only half the truth. Not only is yoga great for improving your general physique, it also gives you a calm and concentrated frame of mind. This is at least as important for a good game of golf as is a healthy and able body.

One of the things yoga focuses on is controlling your breathing. The pressure and competitiveness of a golf game can cause erratic breathing, which makes playing much more difficult. Being able to release all negative thoughts and feelings using yoga techniques will allow you to be focused on the game without any destructive tension.

Physically yoga helps to increase flexibility, in fact a huge proportion of golfers are actually not flexible enough to achieve a really effective swing. As your proficiency in yoga increases, you will become more aware of what your whole body is doing during your swing.

Below we will introduce various poses used in yoga programs aimed at golfers. Main points of focus are on flexibility, on balance and on correcting the posture. The repetitive nature of the golf swing can lead to a body imbalance that yoga can easily correct.

IMPORTANT: Use these exercises we recommend at your own risk. It is recommended that, before beginning any exercise program, individuals seek advice from their physician or a certified exercise professional. The exercises and stretches listed on this web site should be done slowly and carefully. If you feel pain or discomfort STOP IMMEDIATELY!

What Is Yoga?

Yoga is not a recent life philosophy. It has been practiced for thousands of years and during all this time, people benefited from the great results obtained. Furthermore, they conducted investigations, in order to clearly establish the areas in which people can obtain health benefits, by an extended practice. The information obtained after conducting the investigations was grouped in three categories, establishing that yoga practitioners are likely to observe improvements in what concerns physiological, psychological, biochemical aspects.

Various studies revealed that yoga exercises are extremely effective when it comes to increasing the level of joint flexibility, together with the level of lubrication of joints, ligaments and tendons. Another interesting aspect has to do with the fact that yoga is one of the very few techniques, which contributes to massaging all the internal organs and glands, including the ones that are hardly ever stimulated during the lifetime of a person. The stimulation and massaging of the internal organs proves to be beneficial when it comes to preventing and keeping away diseases.

Moreover, these ancient and efficient techniques guarantee a complete detoxification of your body. When stretching the muscles and performing a thorough massage, due to the complexity of the yoga exercises you ensure the optimum quantity of blood supply you need. As a consequence, toxins are eliminated from your body and certain undesired processes, such as aging, are considerably delayed.

As a final remark, all the benefits presented above come in addition to the most important aspect provided by yoga practices, meaning the harmony and the synchronization between body and mind, as well as strengthening your meditation and emotional systems.

Getting Started with Yoga for Golfers

One great thing about getting started in yoga is that it requires no significant investment. In contrast to golf there is not specific yoga training equipment that one has to use in order to obtain the desired results. Unlike golf you also don't need to be at any special place to do your yoga exercises and can do it in the comfort of your home.

All this is a direct consequence of the fact that yoga is, more than a practice, a state of mind and a life style. That is why your will, as well as your believes and attitudes towards this philosophical path are all that actually matter. Moreover, a balanced and healthy diet, based on natural food, is a key issue for preparing yourself for your first yoga session. What we eat can strongly affect both our mind and our soul, so it is crucial to mind what we eat.

Even though you do not need a specially designed place for performing your yoga class, make sure, when electing the room where you will be holding the class, to choose a place as far away from distractions - such as radio, street noise, TV - as possible. The place also needs to be clean and quite and, if possible, ventilated. A blanket or exercise mat is the accessory that you absolutely need in order to gain comfort when carrying out the exercises and the meditation, as they are performed in either sitting or lying positions. Wear something very comfortable and loose, such as training suits, sweat pants and a t-shirt, shorts or loose pajamas.

It is also highly recommended to have an empty stomach before starting your yoga exercises. As a general rule, at least one or two hours after a main meal is a good time for practicing yoga. As breathing is a key element in yoga training, do not forget to also clean your nostrils and your throat.

Yoga exercises can be performed at any time of the day. In fact both morning and evening practices are beneficial to your body and mind. Performing the exercises in the morning can contribute to your good shape for the whole day, as it improves your vitality level. On the other hand, evening yoga practices helps inducing a restful and peaceful sleep.

Your yoga session should not exhaust you. Do not hesitate to take a break when you feel tired. Actually, short breaks are common, especially between difficult exercises. Keep in mind that as little as 15 minutes of correct yoga practice can produce great results on your body and mind, and ultimately your golf game.

Yoga Equipment

The degree of preparation for practicing yoga is minimal. It is true that you have to mind your diet, but mental preparation is by far more important. Still, when it comes to yoga equipment, there are a few things to keep in mind. These things are not mandatory, but recommended in order to increase the level of efficiency and comfort.

1. Yoga clothing: There is no such thing as a strict rule regarding the type of clothes that one has to wear while performing yoga exercises. Nevertheless, practice has demonstrated that comfortable, loose, breathable clothes are the most convenient ones for carrying out this routine. Sweat suits, shorts, pajamas and t-shirts are the outfits people mostly opt for. As for certain exercises from a regular yoga routine your head comes below your knees, you might want to put on a t-shirt that is tight to your body.

2. Shoes: As a general rule, yoga exercises are performed in bare feet. Most of the times, shoes are left near the entrance in case you go for yoga classes. In order to prevent discomforts caused by the cold sensations, you can put on light cotton socks.

3. Mats: Mats are used for various reasons. First of all, they delimitate the personal space dedicated to each person if you take part in a group yoga session. This way every yoga practitioner can try to reach the state of harmony between the mind and the body, within the space allocated to him, space that he can control and dominate. Another relevant reason for using mats is related to the level of comfort. If you sweat your hands might get slippery and you might loose your stability. For that reason a mat can help you stay focused on the routine. Especially if you are a beginner in yoga training, you have to deeply consider purchasing a mat, as the hard floor might be a serious cause of discomfort to you.

4. Blankets: It is common for yoga studios to have enormous piles of blankets. Do not hesitate to grab one or two, as they can turn out to be handy during classes. They can either be used as props, while performing exercises in uncomfortable positions, or you can use them to cover yourself, during relaxation at the end of the class, in case you get chilly.

There are other elements such as blocks and straps, for example, which people use to improve their efficiency and level of comfort, while carrying out the yoga exercises.

Yoga Meditation

Meditation is definitely one of the main principles of yoga, as it has been verified that it is a trustworthy tool to use for achieving mental clarity and health. A very important thing to know is the fact that there are various types of meditation exercises, designed for both the beginner and the advanced yoga students. You should carefully analyze all details and information provided on each and every one of these techniques and exercises, so that you obtain the maximum results from your meditation routines.

Despite the fact that many people believe that, just like breathing, meditation is something that comes naturally and cannot be taught, there are a few aspects of this process which can increase your efficiency and your results. One of the aspects you have to bear in mind is the time of the day when you carry out your yoga meditation It would be perfect if you could do it either in the morning or late in the evening, as during those particular moments of the day, the atmosphere is charged with a high level of spiritual energy.

Here is some advice regarding meditation:

- Before starting the meditation session free your mind of all worries.
- Try to locate a quiet place, where you are not likely to be disturbed.
- It is recommended to choose the same moment of the day, as well as the same place, for your meditation routine.
- Focus on meditation; do not let your mind get lost in other thoughts.
- Try to follow a pattern when breathing.
- Your head, back and neck have to be placed in a perfect straight line.

Remember that it is crucial both to perform the meditation session and to observe the results, in order to get close to experiencing the supreme synchronization between the body and the spirit.

Correct Breathing in Yoga

When carrying out your yoga routine it is not very relevant what you put on or where you perform it, but details such as what you ate that day, the manner in which you breathe and your attitude towards the yoga exercise do have an impact.

Without the proper breathing techniques yoga is no more than a series of acrobatic exercises. In order to explore the full benefits of all yoga practices you have to realize that deep breathing may bring a new sense to the way you perceive your life and actions. The oxygen we inhale helps the body assimilate the nutrients we eat. While exhaling we are eliminating unwanted carbon dioxide that is toxic for our bodies.

Although breathing is an activity that we do not learn how to do, we sometimes restrict or modify the way we perform this action which can only result in negative effects for us. Most yoga practitioners agree that there is a close connection between the mental state and the manner in which a particular person breaths. Thus, in order to achieve the perfect state of harmony between the body and the soul, yoga trainers organize sessions dedicated completely to teaching the proper breathing techniques, which highly contribute to reaching the desired stage of peacefulness and synchronization between the inner and the outer self.

Yoga breathing does not encourage shallow and fast breathing, but tries to promote the benefits of deep breathing. Among the most important beneficial effects of this manner of breathing we can enumerate:

- Improvement of health and brain irrigation systems.
- Rejuvenation of the skin, which becomes considerably smoother, while facial wrinkles are gradually eliminated.
- Deep breathing leads to stronger lungs and to a healthier heart.
- Relaxation of the body and mind.

Anuloma Viloma is a commonly practiced example of an Alternate Nostril Breathing Technique. The yoga practitioner is actually inhaling through one nostril, then he or she has to retain the breath for a few moments and eventually exhale the air through the other nostril.

Here are the six steps to be followed when practicing this technique:

1. Tuck your index and middle finger into your nostrils, in order to close your nostrils. Your thumb should be placed by your right nostril, while your ring finger and little fingers should be by your left. Now you can start inhaling through the left nostril, closing the right one with the thumb, until you count from one to four.
2. Hold your breath, to the count of sixteen.
3. Exhale through your right nostril, to the count of eight, while you close your left nostril with the little fingers.
4. To the count of four, inhale through the right nostril, keeping the left one closed.
5. To the count of sixteen, hold your breath, by closing both nostrils.
6. Exhale though the left nostril, to the count of eight, while keeping the right nostril closed.

Ujjayi is also known as the loud breathing technique, the Ujjayi is performed by breathing through both nostrils while keeping the glottis closed to a degree. This technique is used in order to increase your control over the activity of your lungs. It also functions as a method of clearing the throat. The name comes from the fact that the air passing through the partially closed glottis makes a constant and fluent sound. Yogis try to eliminate nasal sounds and to keep the constant flow of air and sound on a harmonious tone.

In order to correctly practice this breathing method you have to use chin lock and also employ the closure of both nostrils. Keep the pause for as long as you can and gently exhale at the end. The left nostril is usually used to let out the air. In case you kept your nostrils closed with your fingers you can simply release pressure of the left nostril and the air will flow out naturally. Simultaneously with releasing the nostril try to unlock the chin and open the glottis to a higher extent.

Inhaling air should be given half the time you reserve for exhaling. Determining the precise inhalation and exhalation times is different for each person but you will probably find this out yourself while practicing Ujjayi. Holding the pause for a long time between breathing in and out might be difficult to do. In time, however, you will be able to hold the pause as long as the exhalation time.

Sequence of Poses in a Yoga Session

There is a rhythm in the practice of yoga that offers amazing beneficial results, when used correctly. Performing the postures in the right order is essential to finding this rhythm and allowing your body to naturally flow from one stage to the next, without interruptions or abrupt leaps. The beginning pose should be the Corpse pose, which should then be repeated between other poses and as a final relaxation method. The standard yoga pose - the easy pose - is perfect as an energy recharger. It is also a good position for meditation, however while allowing your mind to gain strength, try to mind the position of your back, which should not be arched.

Continuing with the warm up exercises, try to relax your neck muscles. This is important because the neck is the upper point of the central energy line of the body, which is represented by the spine. The shoulder lifts are the natural following exercise. Supplementary you may also try some eye exercises, which improve overall eyesight strength and prevent tiredness. To further prepare for the more difficult postures you can attempt to practice the sun salutation pose, which will stretch all the body muscles. Leg raises will tone your leg muscles, giving you more endurance and improved flexibility, while the head stand pose is also good for resting specific organs in your body - such as the heart. Another variation of this pose is the shoulder stand, which is also beneficial to the spine and lower back muscles.

The bridge and the plough poses increase your back flexibility. Although they might look difficult to perform, both poses are accessible if gentle movements are performed. Do not get discouraged if the perfect stance is not achieved from the first few attempts, as it takes time to develop the strength and flexibility required to execute them correctly. Stimulating the nervous system is also performed by holding the forward bend pose. The fish pose is also rather acrobatic, but it tones the chest muscles and the lungs. The cobra pose stimulates the pelvic and lower abdomen area, improving circulation and massaging the internal organs. This pose is also beneficial to stretch the lower back in order to achieve a greater swing arc for your golf swing.

Strengthening the lower back may be continued with the locust pose, which also has good effects on the abdominal muscles. The locust pose is known to help prevent constipation. The bow is another pose that helps your back area remain flexible and strong at the same time. Abdominal fat may also be reduced while in this pose, especially when a proper diet is adopted. Furthering the exercises for your spine you can try the half spinal twist pose.

Joints and arm strength are improved by the crow pose. This pose also has positive effects on your breathing as it forces the chest area to expand, over time, thus giving you more breathing capabilities. Followed by the hands to feet pose and the triangle, the poses require you to test your body's full strength and flexibility. The final corpse pose allows your body to rest and replenish any energy that might have been lost during the practice.

Now for some more detail:

Leg Raises

The Leg Raise exercises have the purpose of preparing the body for the yoga poses. The particular muscles, which are straightened and toned by these exercises, are the abdominal and lower back muscles, together with the muscles of the legs. You might not have strong muscles and, as a result, you'll find this routine difficult to perform, but, after a while, the moves will be easy to carry out.

If your physical shape is not the best, you are likely to find yourself arching your lower back or using your shoulders to help lift your legs. In order to maximize the effects of the exercises it is very advisable to have the full length of your body resting on the floor, while your shoulders and your back are relaxed. Leg Raises normally begin with the legs together and the palms down on the sides of the body.

You can perform leg raises by either raising one leg, while the other one remains on the floor or by raising both of them, at the same time. If you work only with one leg, you can start by pushing down with your hands, to facilitate the leg lifting. For best results, maintain the knees straight and try to lower your back as down as possible to the floor in order to straighten the spine, as well.

When performing this routine also mind the manner in which you breathe, as it is widely known that deep breathing can contribute to prompt and satisfying results.

The Corpse Pose

The Corpse Pose can either be practiced before or in between Poses, or as the Final Relaxation. Before starting your Corpse Yoga Pose make sure you have laid symmetrically, as you need to have proper space to stretch you hands and your legs. You will notice that once you are done with this exercise you experience a feeling of relaxation of all your muscles.

When working on this pose, it is advisable to start by rotating your legs in and out and letting them fall slowly on the sides. Then, repeat the movement with your hands. The next move implies your spine. Rotate it by turning your head from side to side. Letting gravity embrace you, stretch yourself in a similar manner as if somebody was pulling your head away from your feet. Keep your shoulders down and as away from the feet as possible.

Soon, you will feel your entire weight going deeper into a state of profound relaxation. At this moment breathing is a key element, for obtaining the best results. Thus, you have to make sure you breathe deeply and your whole abdomen is rising when you inhale. Many specialists, as well as yoga practitioners agree that there are a lot of beneficial actions going on in your entire system, when you breathe correctly, such as, for example, removal of stress and reduction of the body's energy loss.

For all its helpful results, the Corpse Pose is highly popular among the relaxation poses.

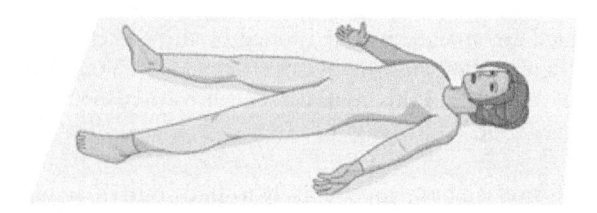

The Easy Pose

The Easy Pose is a relaxation pose and it is normally practiced after the Corpse Pose.

Also known under the name of Sukhpose, the Easy Pose is great for meditation. You only have to sit down on the floor, or on your yoga mat, bend your knees, clasp your arms around them and press them until they reach your chest and your spine erects. Then, release your arms and place your legs in a crossing position, letting your knees fall down to the floor. Make sure you place your hands on your knees and your palms face up.

It is important to keep your head up and the position of your spine as straight as possible. Just as it happens in the case of most of the yoga poses, breathing is important in the Easy Pose, as well. Thus, you have to make sure you fill you lungs with air and hold it as long as it is comfortable. It is advisable to always breathe through your nose. While sited in the Easy Pose, relax your face, your jaws and your belly.

Great for any age group and for frequent practice, the Easy Pose is, however, to be avoided after a chronic or recent knee injury or inflammation, as it might bring you great discomfort. In order to add to your comfort level you can place a folded blanket either under your knees or under your hipbones.

This pose is highly recommended for meditation, as it is not difficult to perform and it promotes inner calm and relaxation.

The Cat Pose

Breath and movement control is essential in all yoga poses, and the Bidal pose is a great exercise to help you get ready. Also known as the Cat Pose, this technique improves coordination and balance. The alignment of the center of your body is closely related to the position of your central area (the pelvic area) in relation with the rest of your body. The central balance point in all poses should be considered your hip area because it is the one dictating the movement and direction of your spine - your central energy line. In the cat tilt pose your hip is bent forward making your spine arch backward. Most yoga poses require you to use either the dog tilt (bending backward) or the cat tilt. Some require you to be neutral while others need a combination of all choices.

The aim of most prone yoga poses is to prepare the body muscles in areas such as strength and flexibility. Muscle stretches don't only improve the way you will perform other yoga poses but also help your organism increase blood circulation. They also stimulate the nerve endings, keeping every portion of your body alive and energetic. Another characteristic of the prone poses is that they require and teach you how to have a straight back and a good yoga posture. Certain poses, such as the leg pull, for example, may seem a bit too demanding at first, so you should not get discouraged if you are unable to follow the instructions all the way from the first attempt.

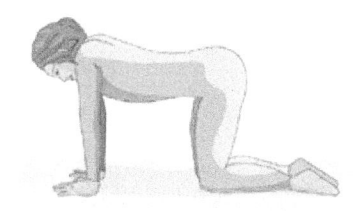

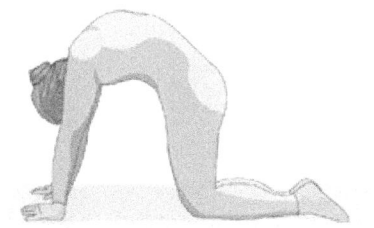

The Cobra Pose

When performing the Cobra Pose, the head and the trunk gracefully arch up. The spine stretches powerfully and the abdominal organs together with the surrounding musculature receive a thorough massage. This pose is extremely recommended for pain and constipation relives, as well as for treating menstrual irregularities.

In order to proceed with the exercise keep your shoulders down and your face relaxed and your elbows tucked to your body. Then lie down with your legs together. It is recommended to place your hand palms under your shoulders and to rest your forehead on the floor.

While inhaling, slowly move your head upwards, brushing first your nose and then your chin against the floor. Then, you need to lift your hands and make use of your back muscles to raise your chest as high as possible. After holding your breath for a few moments, exhale, slowly returning to the initial position.

While inhaling, gradually return to the previous position, only this time it is recommended to use your hands to push the trunk up. Push your body upwards until you are bending from the middle of your spine. Try to hold in that position for as long as two or three breaths and then exhaling, slowly come down.

Raise the trunk as before, inhaling deeply. However, try this time to bend your back until you feel it bending from the neck to the base of our spine. Hold the position for as long as you feel comfortable. Breathing normally, slowly return down to the initial position and relax.

The Bow Pose

The Bow Pose implies raising both halves of your body simultaneously, through a combination of other yoga poses. You have to make use of your hands and arms in order to pull your trunk and legs up together to form a curve. This movement tones your back muscles and contributes to increasing the elasticity of your spine, while also increasing vitality and improving posture. The Bow Pose balances the weight of the body on your abdomen, which reduces abdominal fat. Furthermore your internal organs receive a powerful massage.

In order to proceed with the move you need to lie down comfortably on your front, keeping your head down. Now, while inhaling, bring your knees up and reach back with your hands in order to hold your ankles. Remaining in the same position, exhale. Continue by inhaling, while raising your head and chest and simultaneously pull your ankles up, by lifting both your thighs and knees of the floor. While arching backwards, keep your look up. Maintaining the position, take three slow and deep breaths and then exhale and release your ankles.

In order to exercise the Rocking Bow Pose, you have to first come into the Bow position, and then gradually rock forward and backward. It is recommended to exhale, while rocking forward and to inhale, while rocking backwards. Your head should remain in a static position while you proceed with the Rocking Bow Pose and your look should be up. Normally, you should repeat the rocking up to ten times, and then completely relax your body.

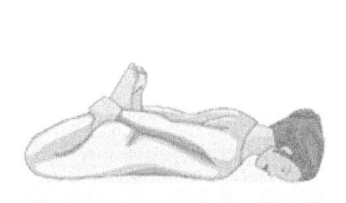

The Shoulder Stand

This pose is considered to be one of the best yoga poses and it is very popular with yoga practitioners. However, this pose must be accompanied by deep breathing, otherwise it will not be more than an acrobatic looking position. The shoulder stand pose was also adopted by gymnasiums and sports training facilities and it can be performed both by men and women with maximum efficiency.

Begin the pose by lying on your back, with the legs straight and close together and the arms parallel with the torso. Raise your legs towards the ceiling, and point your toes upward. Let the weight of your body rest on the neck muscles and on the deltoid muscles of the shoulders. Support the back and legs into the vertical position by allowing your hands to give the lower back the balance it requires. While going into the pose breathe deeply.

Hold the pose with your legs and spine straight. Begin to breathe slowly and deeply while concentrating on the thyroid gland. It is located in the neck area so the shoulder stand will have a profound effect on it, increasing its tone. Hold the pose for a couple of minutes for best effects.

When you are ready to come out of the shoulder stand curve your back and knees simultaneously and lower them to the ground. Remove your hands and place them flat on the floor. When the back is completely flat on the floor, straighten the knees and gently lower the legs.

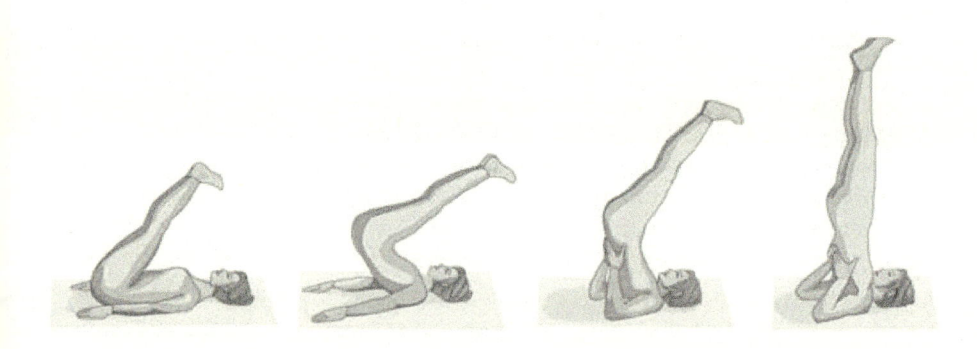

The Fish Pose

The fish pose is the natural successor of the shoulder stand and it is recommended that you practice it as a counter pose to the stand. The pose implies a compression of the spine and neck as opposed to the stretch obtained while in the shoulder stand or Bridge and Plough poses.

There are several benefits of the fish pose. First of all it helps you expand the chest cavity, enabling the lungs to breathe more air and to become more accustomed to deep breathing techniques. The neck muscles and nerves also become stronger and more responsive while the spine increases its flexibility.

Begin the pose by lying down on your back with the legs straight and close together and with the spine kept straight, parallel to the floor. The position of the arms is also important: they should be straight, positioned under your thighs. The palms rest together, stuck to the floor while the elbows are as close to one another as possible.

It is time to go into the pose. Press your elbows down on the floor and arch your back. Take a deep breath as you are doing this. Keeping the weight of your body on your elbows, move your head backwards until it reaches the floor. Exhale while holding the fish pose. Relax your legs and allow your chest to expand while taking in a long breath. In order to come out of the pose try to slowly lift your head and only then release pressure from your elbows.

The Bridge Pose

The bridge pose is usually accomplished while coming down from the shoulder stand pose, with the feet going into the opposite direction. The spine experiences a reverse bend and all neck pressure is relieved. Holding the bridge is beneficial for the back and abdominal muscles. Entering the pose and exiting it also helps develop stronger wrists and a more flexible spine. As a caution you should try to keep your thumbs pointed in the same direction as the shoulder stand, otherwise you risk hurting your fingers.

The first step while performing the bridge pose is to lie on your back and hold your feet together while you keep your knees bent. Just like in the shoulder stand, try to lift your hips as far as possible by placing your hands on the lower back. While in the shoulder stand you become prepared for the bridge - reverse the pose movements until you come out of the shoulder stand pose. After doing this a couple of times go back into the shoulder stand and bend the right leg, while lowering it to the floor.

Bring your left leg down, together with your right. Maintain the pose while inhaling deeply for a few times. Take one deep breath and go into the shoulder stand and then release the pose and come out of it. In time you will notice that lowering both legs simultaneously is also possible. This is a difficult pose if you are lacking spinal flexibility, but it is achievable by anyone willing to invest some time into practicing it.

The Plough Pose

Performing the plough requires you to harmoniously use the flexibility and muscle tone developed with other yoga poses, such as the shoulder stand. Practice will allow you to go in and out of this pose with ease and grace.

From the shoulder stand slowly lower your feet to the floor above your head. The legs should be kept extended at all times and the position of the spinal column should be perpendicular to the floor. Once the toes are stuck to the floor continue to raise your lower back and pelvis towards the ceiling.

The neck and head position are also important. Try to keep your neck relaxed and your muscles soft. Pressing the chin away from your chest will help you achieve this easier. Press your arms down on the floor to give you the support you need to hold the pose. Your hands should keep pressing your lower back area towards the ceiling.

You can bring a variation of this pose by releasing your lower back and moving your hands opposite to the legs, on the floor. Press your palms and lower arm region on the floor as you attempt to have your thighs go as high towards the ceiling as possible.

Exit the pose by bringing the arms to your lower back region and roll out of the pose while exhaling.

The Locust Pose

This pose is excellent for improving the strength of the lower back muscles but it also works well for toning the legs and arms muscles. The Locust is also great for preparing to perform the more difficult bending poses. Do not dismiss this pose as being too simple looking, as it holds various degrees of difficulty that can make it a very challenging and rewarding pose.

While this pose has many beneficial aspects, such as improving posture and back position during standing and walking, it is also advisable to attempt it when your body is in good condition. If you have suffered back or neck injuries you should show extra caution while attempting this pose.

Begin the locust pose by lying on your front side while keeping the hands close to the body. The palms of the hands should be facing up, resting on the floor. Rotate your thighs inward by moving the big toes to face each other. While exhaling move your arms and legs away from the floor. The head and upper body should also move upwards while you are keeping your balance on your belly.

Stretch your arms but remember to keep them parallel to the floor. Press your arms towards the ceiling and raise your head slightly by keeping the base of the head lifted. Holding the pose may become difficult after a while. However, try to hold the Locust pose for about a minute. Come out of the pose while exhaling and then rest for a while and breathe deeply before attempting to go in the pose again.

Yoga Standing Poses

Some of the most efficient poses are the standing positions. They offer excellent stretching of the muscles and they have noticeable effects on the promptness and accuracy of the nervous system. Most standing poses manage to improve the poses and they offer you an increased chance of mastering equilibrium, both physical and mental. In the following paragraphs we will have a look at two of the most important standing poses, the Mountain pose and the Triangle pose.

The mountain pose (known as the Tadpose) got its name from several defining attributes that share the symbols of the mountain. The pose benefits from a high level of relaxed strength and a feeling of invulnerability. Much like a mountain, the person practicing this pose will be surrounded by stillness and will feel a pronounced sensation of balance. The clarity and profound vision offered by this pose enable you to go deeper in your inner feelings and connect with your inner self on a very profound level.

The mountain pose is achieved by keeping the heels slightly apart, so that toes are parallel. Perform a back and forth rocking motion on your toes and gradually come to a complete stop. Lift the ankles in order to consolidate the pose while also tightening the leg muscles. Push your tailbone towards the floor while lifting your pelvic area towards the navel. Your arms should be hanging near your body while you are pressing your shoulder blades backwards.

The obvious positive effects of the mountain pose made it stand at the basis of many other poses. Tadpose implies that the practicing yogi has to learn the meaning of balance and stillness before moving further. For this reason, the mountain pose is one of the best ways to connect with your inner feelings while learning the subtle ways of yoga. The energy channels of the mountain pose traverse your entire body, following the spine, from the back of the neck and down towards the legs.

The next important standing pose is the Triangle pose, or the Trikonpose. This relatively easy pose has a good stretching effect on the spine, giving it a good lateral motion that complements the stretching of other forward poses. The straightness of the knees is vital while performing this pose, as this will allow your movements to be fluent and to stretch all the targeted muscles and organs. Bending to the left and right should be done gradually and fluently. This is one of the yoga poses that is good for preparing the next levels of postures, which are more advanced and harder to accomplish. The stimulation of the spinal nerves is also beneficial and it improves overall body flexibility.

(see next page for illustrations)

In order to enjoy the full benefit of the triangle pose you have to position your body correctly. Your feet should be spread apart while you are pointing to your toes. Try to alternate the pointing motion from your left foot to your right one while keeping a constant rhythm and perfect balance. After you stretch your arms parallel to the ground you should inhale deeply, allowing the energy to strengthen your movements. While exhaling aim to perform a slight bend to either left or right while sliding your hand down your foot. This motion requires a lot of flexibility in the lower back muscles area, so a good warm up session is absolutely necessary before attempting the triangle. Yogis who try this pose often notice the feeling of a lighter body, combined with a sensation of mild heat in the stretched muscles.

Sun Salutation

The Sun Salutation yoga pose is recommended for practitioners of all ages and especially for the ones who cannot dedicate a lot of time to their yoga routine. The reason why this pose is so highly appreciated has to do with the fact that it involves most of the muscle groups, as well as the respiratory system.

In fact, the Sun Salutation is a sequence of twelve yoga positions, linked together by a flowing motion and accompanied by five deep special breaths. Each of the twelve positions contributes to stretching a different part of the body and different muscle groups. Moreover, it helps expanding and contracting the chest in order to regulate breathing.

Specialists and yoga trainers recommend this exercise for the daily routine, as it can contribute in a very efficient way to the flexibility of your spine and joints.

1. The first of the twelve positions require you to stand up with your feet together. Your palms should be in praying position, in front of your chest. Once you make sure your weight is evenly distributed, exhale profoundly.
2. While inhaling, push the arms up, keep the legs straight and relax the neck.
3. While exhaling fold your body forward, press your palms down and try to place your fingertips in line with your toes.
4. While inhaling bring a leg back and place it on the floor. Arch your back and lift the chin.
5. Bring the other leg back and try to support your weight on hands and toes. Keep your chin down and retain your breath, while performing this move.
6. While exhaling, lower your knees and then your forehead, but keep your hips up and make sure your toes are curled under.
7. Lower your hips, while inhaling. Point your toes and bend as back as possible. Your shoulders should be kept down and your legs together.
8. Curl your toes under and, while exhaling, raise your hips. You should end up in a V position. You should push your heels and head down, while keeping your shoulders back.
9. While inhaling, step forwards and place one of your legs between the hands. Keep your chin up, while resting the other knee on the floor.
10. Bring the other leg forward and bend down from the waist keeping your palms on the floor. Exhale.
11. While inhaling, stretch your arms forward and then up and back over your head and try to slowly bend back.
12. Return to the upright standing position, while exhaling, and bring your arms to your sides.

(see next page for illustrations)

The Crow Pose

In the Crow Pose the weight of your body is supported on your elbows, while your hands and head are orientated forward. This pose is not difficult to achieve, if you make sure you bend forward enough to prevent your mind from wandering. By regularly practicing this pose your wrists, arms and shoulders strengthen, while your concentration level is improved and your breathing capacity expands.

In order to proceed with this pose, squat yourself down and bring your arms between your knees. Your palms should be placed down on the floor, in front of your body. Make sure your shoulders are way apart and your fingers are pointing slightly inwards. Once you got to this position, try to bend your elbows out to the sides, converting the backs of your arms into shelves for your knees to comfortably rest on. Your look should be orientated forwards and you should breathe normally.

Once you got to this position try to identify a reference point on the wall or on the floor in front of you, which you will use for focusing. During this phase of the pose breathing plays a crucial role. Thus, it is important to inhale and then to retain your breath. While retaining your breath, try to lean towards the reference point that you previously selected. While doing this make sure you transfer the weight of your body to your hands and you lift your toes up. Exhale and then try to remain in the same position for about three or four deep breaths.

The Forward Bend

This seated pose is one of the basic poses and it provides every yoga practitioner with an easy and relaxing pose. The key to performing the forward bend is to allow your body to embrace the position naturally rather than forcing it to do so. The bend does wonders for your back region but it also helps massage inner organs for better blood circulation.

Start the pose by taking a deep breath and then raising both arms upwards next to your head. Keep your back straight and slowly lean forward and try to catch your feet. The ideal outcome of the pose is when you are able to hold your toes in your hands, for a while. Holding the pose for about half a minute is perfect. However, always try to keep both your back and your legs straight. This requires a lot of flexibility and you may find it impossible to reach your toes. In this case you should try to grab your ankles and thus make the pose easier. While coming out of the pose try to inhale and then stretch your body upwards in the initial position.

The flexibility required to perform this pose is high and it may take weeks or months for a yogi to be able to reach his or her toes and hold the pose in the optimum position. Do not get discouraged if you cannot achieve the perfect pose from the first few attempts and try to gradually work your way to achieving the maximum effects of the forward bend.

Hands to Feet Pose

Similar to the forward bend, the hand to feet pose gives you some of the same excellent benefits. The hamstrings of the legs are fully extended and stretched in this pose and back and spinal flexibility is also increased. Another positive aspect is an increase of blood circulation, especially to the upper body and head. Bending down as far as possible is desired only if the legs are kept straight. The spine's position also needs to remain straight throughout the exercise.

Start the pose with your hands up in the air, palms facing each other. The arms should be close to your ears and will give you a vertical stretch. Also keep the feet next to one another. Erect your spine by pushing your head upwards and stretch your whole body on a vertical scale in the process.

Exhale and bend forward from the median region towards your feet. It is essential not to bend the knees too much as you are doing this. Go as low as you can - but remember to keep the spine straight as well. Grab hold of your toes (or ankles, if you are not flexible enough yet) and then pull your head towards your legs. Advanced yogis manage to touch their shins with their head in this pose. Each exhalation should be the signal for you to go an inch lower or closer to the shins.

While coming out of the pose remember to inhale gently. The movements of entering the pose should be slowly reversed. After a good stretch with your hands above your head you can lower them by your side and relax.

The Half Spinal Twist

Almost all of the yoga poses increase your spinal column flexibility in a forward-backward position, but there are few that give you better lateral flexibility. The half spinal twist does exactly that and it completes the series of poses and exercises that develop mobility and overall fitness. Apart from increasing flexibility this pose also improves the response of the spinal nerves and it helps massage internal organs.

The pose should be carried out while keeping the spine erect and making a sideways circular motion. The shoulders should be kept level as the twist is performed. Balanced breathing is also vital while performing this pose and you should increase the level of twist with each exhalation.

To begin the position sit on your knees while keeping the legs together and resting the buttocks on the sole of your feet. Move your upper body to the right of your feet and lift one leg and place it over the other one. The foot goes right next to the knee of the other leg. The body slowly twists and your hands should follow the position of the torso. During this motion the spine should remain straight for best efficiency.

The next step is to bring your right arm (if the twist is performed towards the left side) on the left knee. Hold the left foot in your hand as your left hand rests behind you. The head should also be involved in the twist, while looking over the left shoulder.

The Head Stand

The Head Stand pose is considered to be one of the most beneficial yoga postures both for the body and the mind. The reverse of gravity contributes to resetting the heart, to improving the blood circulation and releasing back pain.

In order to get to this position you first have to kneel down and rest your weight on your forearms. Make sure to wrap your hands around your elbows and maintain the position for a few seconds. Then, release your hands and place them in front of your body, with your fingers interlocked.

Place the top of your head on the floor, while the back of your head stays in your hands. Thus, the inverted body can have a firm foundation made of the hands and the elbows, which form a tripod. Once you got to this position, you can straighten the knees and slowly raise your hips.

Try to bring your feet in a position as close to your head as possible without bending the knees. Your head should be in a straight line with the spine and your hips should be pulled in such a way that your neck does not bend either backward or forward.

Then, bend your knees into your chest and gradually lift your feet off the floor, while slowly moving the hips backwards. It is recommended to take a short break and not immediately raise the knees higher. Using your abdominal muscles, you are ready to lift your bended knees towards the ceiling. Now you can slowly place your legs in a straight position. Normally, most of the body's weight is felt on the forearms. In order to safely come down in the original position, reverse the steps.

Shoulder Lifts

A high percentage of yoga practitioners declare that they practice yoga for its beneficial results on their health. Thus, many consider yoga a great modality of reducing stress, strengthening the muscles, reaching profound relaxation and improving one's meditation techniques.

Due to the everyday problems and worries, a lot of people have to deal with stress and discomforts. Thus, they realize that it is harder for them to concentrate on things, they become more and more restless and they are unable to relax anymore.

The areas of the body where we inevitably feel the presence of stress are the shoulders and the neck. These parts of our body hold a lot of tension, which produces severe headaches. For that reason, yoga trainers recommend the practice of Shoulder Lifts as many times a day as necessary.

In order to perform these moves you simply have to raise one shoulder at the time or the two shoulders at once and repeat the movement at least five times. Make sure you do it as slowly as possible and you keep your spine straight. Please mind the way you breathe, as a deep breath can maximize the beneficial effects of your exercises.

When slowly practicing the shoulder lift moves you will start to feel relaxed and the tension you feel in your shoulders will gradually go away.

The great thing about these exercises is the fact that one can practice them anywhere, including at work, in front of the TV or during a tiring journey, and the results are always amazing.

Eye Exercises

Yoga practitioners place a great accent on the eye exercises. By working out the eye muscles they are able to prevent any possible problems caused by loss of tone and vitality of these muscles, which usually appear once the person reached maturity. Eye tensions not only reduce the ability of the eye to focus at different distances, but they also cause a great discomfort, due to the fact that the eyes are connected to the brain via the optic nerve.

Eye exercises are recommended not only for preventing eye illnesses, but also for improving the sight and curing minor dysfunctions of the eye. A lot of people are interested in correctly performing these exercises. In order to proceed with eye exercises routine, make sure you are comfortably sited, with your eyes wide open. It is important that your back is in a straight position, your hands are on your knees, your body is relaxed and your head remains straight. During the period you perform the exercises your body should remain in the same position and no part of your body should move except for your eyes.

Choose two reference points: one on the wall and one on the floor and repeatedly raise and lower your eyes on those points. This move represents the warm up for the exercises. Then, once you feel prepared, move your eyes as upwards as possible and then as downwards as you can. It is recommended to repeat the moves 5 times and then blink quickly in order to allow the eyes to relax.

Repeat the exercise, but, this time use reference points placed to your right and to your left, at your eye level. Once you repeated the exercise 5 times, do not forget to let the eye muscles rest.

Kids and Golf

When to get them started

Not so easy to say. I gave my daughter a club and a ball to play with when she was six month old, but all she would use it for was to try and stuff it in her mouth. I would think that generally the best age for a child to begin playing golf would be the time when it can stand securely on the feet while swinging a stick (don't even think about your one-iron yet!). That would be around 2½ years of age or thereabouts. That would also be the age when you can get the child's attention as kids will try out everything the parents do.

How to get them started

To try and teach a three-year old the difference between a "slice" and a "hook" would almost be like Einstein trying to teach you the relativity theory. The main focus is for the kid to have fun. If you are too strict you will most likely spoil their interest. It's okay to let them start by hitting the ball hard, that's part of the fun! Don't worry about their grip right off the bat. Just have them keep the right hand under the left and then swing away! I'd also make sure the child keeps his or her feet on the ground while following through.

Hours of practice will only overwhelm a child, so just allow him or her to practice a little bit at first, say 30 minutes. This will keep motivation for practice high.

For starters, get a toy golf set from your neighborhood toy store, they go for less than $15.00. For older kids, invest not more than $70.00 for a used kids set of usually three pieces: small (7-) iron, small (7-) wood and putter. Buy them according to the size of your kid, and don't buy them if they don't fit.

Take your kid(s) to a grassy area (park, playground etc.) and bring a large empty tin (or something like this). The tin will be the hole - don't dig a hole, you may get into serious trouble with the authorities! Just put the tin onto the grass and explain to your kids that the goal will be to 'bang' the tin with the ball. If you use an object too small kids will have it too difficult to hit it and loose interest. Also, don't use golf balls yet. Screaming "FORE" on a playground will not save you from any law suits if your kids hit somebody unconscious. Now take to your kids some distance away from the tin, for a four-year old not more than 25m, for a seven-year old not more than 120m. If too far they need too many shots and again loose interest. To your older kid you can probably explain some basics of hitting. A

198

small kid will probably just hit the ball, run after it, hit it again, run after it and so on, until the ball bangs the tin (sounds a bit like my own game, too).

Little contests and games keep motivation high. Avoid pressure or competition early on. You want your child to enjoy the game and want to play it every chance they get, not end up so confused and unfocused that they can't figure out what to do and just quit in frustration.

If you're encouraging, your child will love for you to play alongside of them. Just don't start demanding wins and emphasizing competition, or you'll pop the enthusiasm really fast. Children will move along as they're ready. Letting them progress at their own pace prevents future burnout. Never make a child play the game, unless he wants to. The game should be fun, and a simple joy. Laugh and have a blast yourself!

If your child's interest increases, you might consider golf camp or some private lessons with someone experienced in teaching children. If you do seek a personal instructor for your child, watch how the person teaches first. You really want an encouraging person with a knack for teaching kids.

Slowly explain some of the basic rules, as well as some basic etiquette. Tell the kids they can not run wild at the club house (although I've seen plenty of that). Don't talk while someone else is swinging. Don't step in front of someone while they're swinging. Stand still. Don't walk in front of someone else's line or through line.

Take them to the Course

Once the kids get a hang of it and still like it, take them to your golf course (check with your course first, some may not allow kids. If so, write a nasty letter to the management!). Under close supervision, let them play on the putting green and take them to the range. There you can teach them the basics like proper stand and so on, you know the drills. One day when there's not much crowd, take the kids for a nine hole game. Put up their own T-box close enough to the green so they don't get frustrated. Even a nine year old will give up on a 560m par five. Let them T-off at 100 to 150 m from the green. They can at this point also learn how to keep a score card.

Never criticize. Praise their shots and swings. Encourage them to correct certain moves, but don't dwell on what was done incorrectly. Make the whole thing a family outing, but don't start any competition yet. The most important thing is: Keep it fun (and don't ask your kid to wager his/her pocket money on a game).

Golf Glossary

There are so many terms in golf that it's impossible to include all of them in this book. Below are just some of the terms you will encounter as you become more involved with this game:

Ace: A hole-in-one. To sink the ball into the hole right from the tee-off.

Acceleration: An increase in speed most often associated with the hands, arms or club.

Address: The position taken by a golfer as he is about to hit the ball.

Advice: Instructions on how to play a ball.

Aggregate: The total score of members of a team. In a multi-round competition, the total score of each round.

Aiming: The act of aligning the clubface to the target.

Air Shot: A golf shot that misses the ball completely.

Albatross: A score of three strokes under par. Also called a 'Double Eagle'.

Alternate Ball: A competition format in which players take alternate turns to hit the ball. Also called Foursomes.

Amateur: A golfer who plays without cash rewards.

Angle Of Approach: The angle at which the club moves downward towards the ball.

Approach Shot: A shot designed to send the ball to the putting green.

Apron: The piece of ground surrounding the putting green.
Also called the fringe (see picture on right)

Attack: An aggressive play.

Attend The Flag: Action of holding the flag and then removing it while another golfer plays.

Away: The ball that is farthest from the hole when there are two or more.

Back Door: The back end of the hole.

Back Lip: The sloping part of a bunker farthest to the green.

Back Nine: Holes #10 through #18.

Baffle: A 5-wood.

Ball at Rest: A ball that is not moving.

Ball Embedded: A golf ball that is stuck into the ground

Ball Holed: A ball that has gone completely below the level of the lip of the hole.

Ball In Play: A ball is in play once the player has made a stroke on it at the tee box. It remains in play until it is holed out, lost, out of bounds, lifted or substituted.

Ball Marker: Anything that is used to indicate the position of a golf ball.

Ball Retriever: A long pole with a scoop at the end that is used to fetch a ball

Ball Washer: A machine for cleaning golf balls (see picture on the right).

Banana Ball: A ball that curves a lot to the right in the shape of a banana.

Baseball Grip: A grip that utilizes all ten fingers.

Bend One: To curve a ball.

Bent grass: A hardy and resilient grass of the *genus Agrostis* that is native to North America and Eurasia.

Bermuda: A type of grass of the genus *Cynodon dactylon* that is native to southern Europe.

Best Ball: 1. A match in which one player plays against the better score of two balls or the best score of three players.
2. The better score of two partners in a four-ball or best-ball match.

Better Ball: A match play or stroke play game where two players on one side play their own ball throughout the round. The low score or better ball among the two on each hole is the team's score for a hole.

Birdie: A score of one score under par for a hole.

Blade: 1. The clubhead of a golf iron apart from the hosel.
2. To strike the ball with the leading edge of the blade of an iron.

Blade Putter: A putter with its basic head form similar to the other standard irons (see picture on right).

Blast: 1. A powerful drive or an aggressive shot.
2. The action of the club spraying a large amount of sand in a bunker. Also called "explode".

Blind Bogey: A competition format in which each player tries to score closest to a random score.

Blind Hole: A hole on the putting green that is not visible to the player.

Block: A poor shot that is struck late in the swing.

Bogey: A score of one over par for the hole.

Bogey Competition: A competition format where players play against a fixed score at each hole.

Bounce: The angle of the leading edge of a club's sole and the ground. Bounce is most commonly applied to wedges (see picture on the right).

Boundary: The edge of a golf course.

Bowker: A lucky shot that is going astray but hits something such as a tree, rock or spectator, and bounces back into play.

Bramble: A molded surface used on early golf balls.

Brassie: A former name given to a 2-wood. The hitting surface is made of brass.

Break: 1. To score less than a specified number. Eg. "Try to break 90."
2. The turning point of a ball rolling on a slope on a green.
3. The bending of the wrists during a swing.

Bulge: The curved surface of a wood club.

Bulger: A wood club with a curved surface such as a driver.

Bump & Run: A shot in which the ball bounces and rolls some distance.
Bunker: A depression in the ground that is covered with sand. Also called a 'sand trap'.

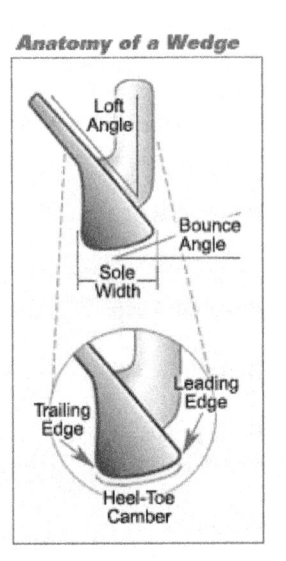

Buried Ball: A ball that is either partially or fully covered by the sand in a bunker.

Caddie: A person who carries a player's clubs and offers advice.

Caddie Master: A person who is in charge of the caddies.

Can: To make a putt.

Card: 1. To make a score. 2. A golfer's score card.

Carpet: A slang term referring to the putting green or fairway in a golf course.

Carry: The distance traveled by a golf ball before it touches the ground.

Cart : A vehicle used to transport golfers and their equipment on the course.

Casting: A premature uncocking or unhinging of the wrists on the downswing. Also known as 'hitting from the top'.

Casual Water: A temporary accumulation of water usually caused by rain or a water sprinkler. This is not a hazard and a player is allowed to lift his ball and play from another spot without penalty.

Center Shafted: A putter in which the shaft is joined to the center of the head.

Charge: 1. To come from behind. 2. To play aggressively.

Chicken Wing: A swing flaw where the left elbow (for a right-hander) bends at an angle pointed away from the body.

Chili-Dip: To strike the ground before the ball during a chip shot.

Chip Shot: A short low approach shot.

Chip-And-Run: A chip shot that enables the ball to roll some distance on the green. Also known as "bump and run".

Chip In: To send the ball with a chip shot into the hole

Choke: 1. To grip a club farther down the handle.
2. A slang used to indicate a failed performance under pressure.

Chop: To hit the ball with a quick downward motion.

Chunk: To strike the ground well behind the ball.

Claggy: A lie that is a bit wet and muddy.

Claim: In match play, a protest by a player concerning a possible breach of the rules.

Cleat : The spike on the sole of a golf shoe (see picture on the right)

Cleek: 1. A narrow-bladed iron used for long shots from the rough or sand
2. A name for the 4-wood or 1-iron.

Closed Face: When the clubface is pointed toward the left of the target.

Closed Stance: A position of the player whose leading foot is nearer the target line during address.

Club: 1. The implement used to strike the golf ball consisting of the grip, the shaft & the head.
2. An organization or association of golfers.

Clubface: The hitting area of the club.

Club Professional : A professional who works for a golf club as a teacher and equipment supplier and plays only in local events.

Clubhouse: The main building on the golf course.

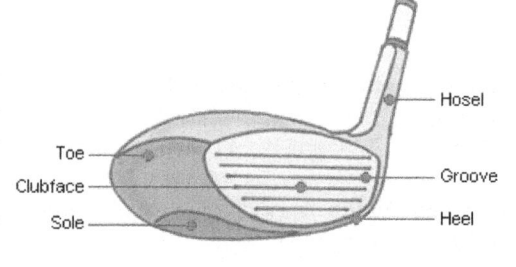

Clubhouse Lawyer: A derogatory term used for a person who appoints himself as an arbiter of the rules.

Cock: To bend the wrists backwards in the backswing.

Coefficient Of Restitution (COR): The ratio of the clubhead speed at impact to the velocity of the ball after it has been struck. The USGA imposed a limit of 0.83 on the COR in 1998.

Collar: The grassy fringe or apron surrounding the putting green.

Colorball: A team game with teams of 3-4 players where one player plays with a colored ball. The score for the team is the sum of the colored ball's score and the best score of the others. For the next hole, another player plays the colored ball. The order of play of the colored ball is decided before the competition.

Come Back Shot: A shot played after overshooting the hole.

Committee: The name given to the group of people in charge of a competition or a course.

Compression: **1.** The deformation of the ball against the clubface on impact.
                     2. The degree of resilience of a golf ball.

Condor: A near impossible hole-in-one shot that can only happen in a par-5 hole. Also called a 'triple eagle'.

Control Shot : A shot that is played with less than full power.

Core: The center of the golf ball.

Course: The entire playing area for the game of golf.

Course Rating: A number expressed in strokes and decimal fractions of a stroke that indicates the number of strokes an average scratch player will take to complete a round from a given tee.

Crack: A condition in which a player's play deteriorates under pressure.

Cross-Bunker: A lengthy bunker that lies across the fairway.

Cup: The container in the hole that holds the flagstick in place.

Cut : A score that reduces the field to a pre-determined number; usually determined after half the number of required holes to be played in a tournament. To remain in a tournament, a player's score must be equal or lower than the cut.

Cut Shot : A controlled shot that makes a ball stop almost instantly on the green.

Dawn Patrol: Golfers who tee off early in the morning to avoid heavy traffic.

Dead: A description of a shot that stops immediately when it lands.

Dead Ball: A ball that is so close to the hole that there is no doubt it will be holed with the next putt.

Deep-Faced Club: A club with a clubface that is relatively thick from top to bottom.

Deuce: A hole made in two strokes.

Dew Sweepers: The first groups of golfers on the course in the morning.

Dimple: Indentation on the golf ball designed to improve its aerodynamics.

Divot: A piece of turf removed by the club when a shot is made.

Dogleg: A bend in the fairway.

Dormie: In match play, a situation in which a golfer is ahead by as many holes that remain. Sometimes spelled 'dormy'.

Double Bogey: A score of two over par for a hole.

Double Eagle: A score of three under par for a hole. Also called an 'albatross'.

Down: The number of holes or strokes a player is behind an opponent.

Downhill Lie: A position of the ball on a slope in which a right-handed golfer's left foot is lower than his right foot.

Downswing: The downward movement of a golfer's club toward the ball.

DQ'd: Short form of the word 'disqualified'.

Draw: 1. The pairing of golfers for a match play.
2. A controlled shot that curves from right to left for a right-handed player.

Drive: To hit a golf ball a long distance, usually with a driver.

Driver: The longest hitting club used primarily from the tee. Also known as the "1-wood".

Driving Iron: An iron club with a loft of approximately 17 degrees, a lie of approximately 56 degrees and a length of 39 inches. Also called a "One iron".

Driving Range: A place with facilities for golfers to practice.

Drop: To put a ball in play on the course after it has been declared unplayable or has been lost.

Dub: A missed or poorly hit shot.

Duff: To mishit the ball by striking the ground behind the ball first.

Duffer: An unskilled golfer. Also called a 'hacker'.

Dunk: To hit the ball into a water hazard.

Eagle: Two strokes under par for a hole.

Equator: The center line of a ball

Equipment: Anything used, carried or worn by a player. A ball in play is not considered equipment.

Etiquette: A set of guidelines to promote proper behavior on the course.

Executive Course: A golf course consisting mainly of par threes and very short par fours.

Explode: The action of the club spraying a large amount of sand in a bunker. Also called a "blast".

Explosion Shot: A shot out of a bunker that takes a great deal of sand with it. *See picture.*

Extra Hole: A hole played after a regulation round or match to break a tie.

Face: The hitting area or surface of the club.

Fade: A controlled shot in which the ball curves slightly from left to right when hit by a right-handed golfer.

Fairway: The area of the course between the tee box and the green that affords a good lie for the ball.

Fairway Wood: A wood club designed to hit the ball off the fairway.

Fan: To swing and completely miss the ball.

Fat Shot: A shot in which the club hits the ground before it hits the ball.

Feather: To hit a shot that lands lightly on the green with little roll.

Featherie: An early handcrafted golf ball made of stuffed feathers wrapped with leather.

Field: Players in a tournament.

Flag: Short for flagstick.

Flagstick: The removable marker placed in the hole to show its location.

Flange: The base of a club or the part that rests on the ground.

Flash Trap: A small, shallow sand trap.

Flat Swing: A swing in which the club is carried back at a relatively low angle to the ground.

Flex: The degree a club's shaft bends upon impact with the ball.

Flier: A shot hit with little or no spin that travels farther than normal.

Flier Lie: A ball sitting on top of the grass in a rough.

Flight: 1. The trajectory of a ball in motion.
2. A division of players of relatively equal standard in a tournament.

Flip Shot: A short shot of high trajectory played with a highly lofted club.

Flub: A poor shot caused by hitting the ground before the ball.

Follow-Through: The part of the swing after the ball has been struck.

Fore: The standard warning call in golf to those in danger of being hit by a ball.

Forecaddie: A person employed by the course or tournament committee to mark the position of a player's ball.

Four-Ball: A match in which the better ball of two players is played against the better ball of their opponents.

Foursomes: A match between two teams of two players each. Each team plays one ball with partners alternating shots.

Free Drop: A ball dropped without penalty into another area.

Fried Egg: A lie in which the ball is buried in sand.

Fringe: An area surrounding the putting green. Also called an 'apron'.

Frog Hair: Short grass bordering the edge of the green.

Front Nine: Holes #1 through #9. Also called "Front side".

Full House: A game in which a player is set a points target calculated by deducting his handicap from 36. The winner is the player who surpasses his target by the most points. Score is 8 points for an eagle, 4 for a birdie, 2 for a par and 1 for a bogey.

Gallery: Spectators of a golf tournament or the area for spectators.

Gimmie: A short putt that is likely to be conceded by the opponent.

Glove: A hand item worn by a golfer to improve the grip.

Goose Neck: A club in which the neck is slightly curved so that the heel is offset from the line of the shaft.

Graphite: A light carbon based material used to make shafts and clubheads.

Grain: The direction in which the grass on the green is growing.

Grand Slam: Winning all four major tournaments: British Open, US Open, PGA Championship and the Masters.

Grasscutter: A hard-hit low flying shot.

Green: Commonly used for the well-defined area where the hole is located.

Green Committee: Members of a golf club overseeing the management and maintenance of the course.

Green Fee: Payment to be made for the use of a golf course.

Green In Regulation: The number of shots taken when the ball stops on the green that is two less than the par of the hole.

Green Jacket: The mantle of honor given to the winner of the US Masters.

Greenkeeper: Employee of a club in charge of course maintenance.

Grip: 1. The area of the shaft where the club is held.
2. The manner in which a player grasps and holds the club.

Groove: 1. The path through which the club travels in a consistent swing
2. Line scored on the face of a club.

Gross: The number of strokes played by a golfer before deducting his handicap.

Ground Under Repair (GUR): The area of the course that is being repaired. A ball lying in this area can be lifted without penalty (see picture below)

Ground the Club: To touch the head of the ground on the ground during address.

Gutta Percha: The rubbery material used to make golf balls from 1948 until early 1900.

Guttie: A golf ball made of gutta percha.

Hack: 1. To strike violently at the ball.
2. To make bad shots.
3. To play bad golf.

209

Hacker: An unskilled golfer. Also called a 'Duffer'.

Half / Halved: When the score is tied on a hole in match play.

Handicap: The number of strokes a player may deduct from his actual score. Designed to allow golfers of different abilities to compete on the same level.

Handicap Certificate: A document issued by a player's home club or golf association that indicates his current handicap

Handicap Golfer: An amateur golfer whose average score is above par and who is given a handicap in amateur competitions.

Hanging Lie: A ball resting on a downhill slope.

Hazard: A well-defined area in a golf course that is designed to make play more difficult.

Head: The part of the club that comes into contact with the ball.

Heel: The part of the clubhead that is closer to the player.

Hickory: Wood from a native North American tree. Used for making club shafts at the beginning of the 19th century.

Hit: To strike a golf ball.

Hitting From The Top: See 'Casting'.

Hog's Back: A ridge of ground or a hole having a ridge on a fairway.

Hold: To hit the ground and stay in place with little roll or bounce.

Hole: 1. A 4¼" (108 mm) round receptacle in the green, at least 4" deep.
2. A defined area starting from the tee box to the green.

Hole High: A ball that is even with the hole, but off to one side.

Hole In One: A hole made with one stroke. Same as an 'Ace'.

Hole Out: To complete play on a hole by hitting the ball into the cup.

Holed: The rules of golf state that a ball is only considered 'holed' when it lies within the circumference of the hole and is entirely below the level of the lip.

Home Green: The green on the last hole of the course.

Home Pro: A professional who holds a position at a golf club, teaches, and plays only in local events

Honor: The privilege of teeing off first on the tee box. This goes to the winner of the preceding hole. On the first tee, this is usually decided by drawing lots.

Hook: An uncontrollable ball that curves from right to left for a right-handed player.

Hosel: The part of the clubhead where the shaft is fitted.

Hustler: A skilful golfer who deliberately maintains a higher handicap than he's entitled to win bets.

In: The second 9 holes on a course – holes 10 to 18.

In Play: A ball that is not out of bounds.

Impact: The instantaneous moment when the clubhead meets the ball.

Inside: Being nearer the hole than the ball of your opponent.

Interlocking Grip: A grip in which the left little finger is intertwined with the right index finger for a right-handed golfer.

In The Leather: A putting distance not greater than the leather wrapping on the player's grip to the clubhead. In friendly play, players often concede such putts.

Intended Line: The line a player expects his ball to travel when hit.

Iron: One of the number of clubs with heads made of iron or steel.

Jerk: To hit the ball out of a bad lie with a downward cutting motion.

Jungle: Heavy rough.

Kick: An unpredictable or erratic bounce of the golf ball.

Lag: A long putt with the intention of getting the ball near the hole so that it can be holed with the next putt.

Lateral Hazard: A hazard that runs parallel to the line of play, usually alongside the fairway.

Lay Up: To hit a safe shot that stops short of a hazard.

Leading Foot: The foot nearer to the target. The left foot for a right-handed player (see picture on right).

Leading Hand: The hand nearer to the target. The left hand for a right-handed player.

Leader Board: A display of the leading golfers and their scores during a tournament.

Lie: The position of a golf ball when it comes to rest.

Line: The path to be traveled by a golf ball.

Line Up: To determine the direction the ball should travel.

Links: Originally referred to a seaside course, but now refers to any golf course.

Lip: The upper rim of the hole.

Lob Shot: A shot that makes the ball go maximum height and minimum distance. Used when a player has to hit over an obstacle and has very little green to work with.

Local Rules: Rules established for a club by its own members.

Loft: 1. The angle between the clubface and the vertical.
2. The height of the ball when it is hit into the air.

Long Game: The part of the game where distance is important.

Long Irons: Irons with lesser loft that hit the ball lower and farther.

Loose Impediment: Natural objects that are not fixed, growing or sticking to the ball. Examples of loose impediments are leaves, twigs, insects and stones.

Lost Ball: A ball is considered lost if:

- It can't be found within five minutes after search begins.
- The player declares it lost before the five minutes of search.
- The player can't identify a ball which is found within five minutes as his.

LPGA: The Ladies' Professional Golf Association.

Make The Cut: To qualify for the final rounds of a tournament.

Mallet: A putter that has a head that is much wider and heavier than that of a blade putter.

Marker: A small object used to mark the spot before it is lifted.

Markers: Objects placed at the teeing ground to define the area in which players must tee their balls.

Marshal: A tournament official whose duty is to keep order among the spectators.

Match Play: A competition format that is determined by the number of holes won instead of the number of strokes.

Meadowland: A lush grassland course.

Medal Play: A competition decided by the overall number of strokes used to complete the round or rounds. Same as 'stroke play'.

Middle Wedge: An iron with a loft that is between that of a pitching wedge and a sand wedge.

Mid-Iron: A middle range iron, usually #5 through #7.

Mis-Club: To use the wrong club for the shot.

Mis-Hit: A term used when the clubhead did not hit the ball correctly.

Mis-Read: To read the line of putt wrongly. Mis-reading the green is a very common thing among all golfers.

Mixed Foursome: A foursome with each side consisting of a male and female player.

Model Swing: A completely professional swing.

Muff: To mis-hit a shot.

Mulligan: A special allowance where a player can replay a shot. Mulligans are not allowed in a proper tournament, but are popular in charity or social tournaments where players can purchase any number of them during a round.

Municipal Course: A public course owned by local government.

Nassau: A 3-part wager comprising of the front nine, the back nine and the complete round of 18 holes.

Neck – The part where the shaft of the club joins the head.

Net: A player's score after deducting his handicap.

Nine: A series of 9-holes.

Nineteenth Hole: The bar at the clubhouse.

Observer: An official who watches the competitors in a tournament and reports any breach of rules to the referee.

Obstruction: An artificial object that obstructs play.

Off-Centre: A ball that is not struck at the center of the clubface.

Offset: A club with its head set behind the shaft.

One Up: A match play term meaning a player has won one hole more than his opponent.

One-Iron: An iron club with a loft of approximately 17 degrees, a lie of approximately 56 degrees and a length of 39 inches. Also called a 'driving iron'.

One-Putt: To hole the ball with just one stroke of the putter when on the green.

One-Wood: Another name for a driver.

Open: A tournament where both amateurs and professions can participate.

Open Stance: A position during address where the front foot is farther from the target line than the back foot. This stance is often used to play a fade ball.

Out: The front nine holes – holes #1 through #9.

Out Of Bounds (OB): The region which lies outside a well-defined boundary. A player is prohibited to play in this region for that particular hole. A penalty is imposed on a player who hits a ball out of bounds. (See Rules).

Outside Agency: Anything that is not part of the match or anyone not part of the competitors' side in stroke play such as observers, forecaddies and referee.

Over Clubbing: To use a club which gives more distance than intended.

Over Par: A score higher than the indicated par for a hole or a round.

Overlapping Grip: A grip used by a player when the little finger of his trailing hand overlaps the space between the forefinger and the second finger of his leading hand. Also called the "Vardon Grip".

Pair: 1. Two golfers playing together in a competition.
2. To assign players to form a team partnership in match play.

Par: The number of strokes a scratch player should take to complete a hole. The course par is the total of all the hole pars.

Parkland: A course laid out in grassland with little rough.

Partner: 1. One of two or more players on the same team in a match
2. A player who plays together with another in a match.

Peg: A golf tee.

Penalty Stroke: An additional stroke added to a player's score for a breach of the rules.

PGA: Professional Golfers Association.

Pick Up: To take the ball before holing out. In match play, the player concedes the hole to his opponent. In stroke play, the player is disqualified.

Pin: A flagstick.

Pin-High: See 'Hole-High'.

Pin Placement: The location of the hole on a putting green.

Pin Position: Same as 'Pin Placement'.

Pitch: A shot that sends the ball high toward the green.

Pinsetter: The person who is responsible for pin placement.

Pitch And Run: A type of pitch shot that is lower and with less backspin that enables the ball to roll more after it lands on the green.

Pitching Niblick: An obsolete name for the 8-iron.

Pitching Wedge: An iron with a heavy flange designed to hit balls high.

Pivot: The act of rotating the hips, truck and shoulders during a swing.

Play-Off: The process of playing additional holes to determine the winner of a competition that ends in a tie.

Play Through: To overtake a group of golfer playing ahead. Golf etiquette dictates that a slower group should signal a faster group to play through.

Playing Professional: A professional golfer who primarily competes in tournaments

Plugged Lie: A lie in which the ball is buried in sand.

Plus Handicap: A player whose average is less than par. During a tournament, an amateur must add strokes to his gross to determine his net score.

Pop Up: A short, high shot.

Pot Bunker: A small deep sand trap that has steep sides.

Practice Green: A green set up for putting practice.

Preferred Lie: Under local rules, a manner in which a player is allowed to improve his lie without incurring a penalty.

Press: An extra bet on the remaining holes of a round.

Pro Shop: A shop at the golf club where golfing equipment is sold.

Pro-Am: A tournament where a professional is partnered with an amateur.

Professional: A player who plays for money. Abbreviated to 'Pro'.

Provisional Ball: A second ball played immediately after the first if the player thinks his first ball may be out of bounds or lost. If the first ball is found or found to be in play, it is played. Otherwise, the player continues to play with the provisional ball.

Pull: A shot that sends the ball relatively straight, but to the right of the target for a right-handed player.

Punch: A low, controlled shot hit into the wind.

Putt: A shot played toward the hole when the ball is on the putting green.

Putter: A club specially designed for putting.

Putting Green: The defined area that is specially prepared for putting.

Putting Surface: Same as 'Putting Green'.

Quail High: A shot that has a low and flat trajectory.

Quarter Shot: A shot that is made with less than a half swing.

Quitting On The Ball: Not hitting through the shot.

R & A: The Royal and Ancient Golf Club of St Andrews who oversees golf in Europe, Asia and the Commonwealth.

Rabbit: A touring professional who has to compete in qualifying rounds in order to play in tournaments.

Rake: A device used for smoothing the sand in a bunker.

Range: A practice area.

Recover: To play back into a satisfactory position on the fairway or green after hitting into an undesirable position.

Recovery Shot: A shot that is recovered. See above.

Release: The movement of a golfer's hands during a swing.

Relief: To drop the ball with penalty in accordance with the rules.

Reverse Overlap: For a right-handed player, a putting grip in which the index finger of his right hand overlaps the little finger of his left.

Rifle: To play a long distance shot with great accuracy.

Rim: The edge of the cup.

Rim Out: To run around the edge of the cup and fail to fall in.

Roll-On-A-Shot: Too much turning of the wrist at impact.

Rough: Long grass next to the fairway or hazards.

Round: A series of 18 holes.

Round Robin: A tournament in which each player plays against each other.

Rub Of The Green: A deflection or stopping of the ball in play caused by an outside agency, and for which no relief is given. In other words, bad luck.

Run: The distance the ball rolls on the ground.

Running Iron: A club used for making short running shots.

Run-Up: An approach shot that is close to or on the ground.

Sandbagger: A person who lies about their ability to gain an edge in the game – in other words, a cheat.

Sand Iron: An early heavy lofted club that was used for playing from bunkers. No longer in use.

Sand Trap: Another name for a bunker.

Sand Wedge: An iron with a heavy flange on the bottom that is specially designed to get the ball out of bunkers.

Sandy Par: Making par from a bunker.

Scoop: An improper swing with a digging or spooning action.

Scotch Foursome: A match where partners take alternating turns at shots. Each hole is started alternatively as well.

Scramble: A team competition in which every team members play from the position of the best ball of a team member after every stroke.

Scratch: A player without a handicap or whose handicap is zero.

Scratch Player: A golfer who does not require a handicap. All professional golfers are scratch players.

Second Ball: A situation can arise where a question over the legality of the ball in play cannot be settled by a referee or other members of the group. In this case, a second ball is played. The play completes that hole with two balls. The score of whichever ball is deemed legal at a post-match adjudication is used.

Scruff: To mishit the ball by grazing the ground with the clubhead before hitting the ball.

Semi-Private Course: A course that has members but is open to the public.

Set: A collection of golf clubs.

Set-Up: The series of preparations a player takes before his swing.

Shaft: The part of the golf club that is connected to the head.

Shag Bag: A bag for carrying practice balls.

Shagging: To collect balls from a practice area.

Shank: A shot struck by the club's hosel.

Shiperio: Similar to a mulligan, but the player is allowed to choose which ball to continue for the rest of the hole.

Short Game: The part of the game consisting of pitching, chipping and putting.

Short Irons: The higher lofted irons; usually from #8 through the wedges.

Shotgun: A tournament where all players start at different holes and at the same time. The origin of such a tournament may have been started by the firing of a shotgun.

Shot Hole: A par three hole.

Shotmaker: A player who has the ability to play a variety of shots.

Shotmaking; Playing a variant shot that warrants the given situation.

Side: A team.

Side hill Lie: A lie with the ball either above or below your feet.

Single: A match involving two players, one against the other.

Sink A Putt: To the ball into the hole.

Skins: A betting game in which the player with the lowest score on a hole wins the pot. If two or more players tie at the lowest score, the pot is carried over and added to the pot for the next hole.

Skull: To hit the ball above its center, usually on a chip or a bunker shot, causing it to travel too far.

Sky: To hit too much underneath the ball sending it much higher than intended.

Skywriting: A bad swing in which the clubhead makes a loop at the top of the backswing and comes down with disastrous results.

Slice: An uncontrollable shot that curves strongly to the right.

Slope: Gradient of the ground.

Slope Rating: A measurement of the difficulty of a course for bogey golfers relative to the **course rating**.

Slump: A period of bad play.

Smother: To hit down on the ball so that it travels a short distance on the ground.

Snake: A very long putt that travels over several breaks in the green.

Snap-Hook: To hit a hot with an acute hook.

Snipe: A ball that is hooked and drops quickly.

Sole: The bottom of the clubhead.

Sole Plate: The metal plate on the bottom of woods.

SPGA: Senior Professional Golf Association.

Spike Mark: A mark made on the green by the cleats of a golf shoe.

Spot Putting: A method of putting in which the player aims at a spot instead of directly at the hole.

Spray: To hit the ball erratically.

Spring: The flexibility of the club shaft.

Square Stance: Placing your feet in a line parallel to the direction you which the ball to travel.

Stableford: A tournament scoring method that uses points instead of strokes.

Stance: The position of a player's feet during his address.

Starter: A person who determines the order of play from the first tee.

Stick: The pin in the hole.

Stimpmeter: An instrument for measuring the speed of greens. It's a 30-inch aluminum trough raised to a 20-degree angle. A golf ball is placed on top of the trough and released to roll down on to the green. The distance it rolls after leaving the trough is then converted to a Stimp reading.

Stipulated Round: The number of holes to be played as determined by the committee during a competition.

Stony: To hit a ball close to the flagstick.

Straightaway: A hole having a straight fairway.

Straight-Faced: A club with little or no loft on the face.

Strike Off: To drive from the tee.

Stroke: A swing at the ball with the intention of hitting it.

Stroke & Distance: A penalty in which one stroke is added to the player's score, and he has to play the shot again from where he last played.

Stroke Play: A competition in which the total number of strokes for one round, or a pre-determined number of rounds, determines the winner

Stymie: When an object such as a tree lies between a player's ball and the green.

Sudden Death: When the score is tied after completing the round in a match or stroke competition, play continues until one player wins a hole.

Summer Rules: Ordinary play according the Rules of Golf.

Surlyn: Material from which most golf balls are made.

Swale: A shallow depression or dip in the ground.

Sweet Spot: The preferred spot on the clubface with which to strike the ball.

Swing: The action of striking the ball.

Swing Weight: Measurement of a club's weight.

Tap In: A very short putt.

Tee: 1. A small device used to elevate the golf ball from the ground.
2. The area in which the ball is place for the first shot of a hole.

Tee Off: To play a tee shot.

Tee Up: To begin play by placing a ball on the tee.

Tee Box: The rectangular area within which a player must place his ball. It is defined by the markers and two club lengths behind them.

Tee Shot: A shot played from a tee.

Teeing Ground: Same as 'Tee Box'.

Temporary Green: A green used in the winter to save the permanent green.

Texas Wedge: What the putter is called when it used from off the green. Also a shot played with a putter from outside the putting green.

Thin: A shot in which the ball is hit above center when the head of the club is following too high a line.

Thread: To play the ball through a narrow opening.

Three Ball: A game where three players compete against each other

Three-Putt: Taking three putts to hole the ball

Threesome: 1. A group of three players playing together.
2. A two against one match with the two partners playing alternating strokes against a single player.

Tight Fairway: A narrow fairway.

Toe: The part of the club farthest from where in joins the shaft.

Toe Job: A shot hit too close to the toe of the club.

Top: To hit the ball above its center causing it to roll or hop on the ground.

Topspin: The forward rotation of the ball.

Touch Shot: A delicate shot of great accuracy.

Tour: A series of tournaments for professionals.

Tournament: A competition in which a number of golfers compete.

Trap: A sand or grass hazard.

Trajectory: The flight path of the ball.

Triple Bogey: A score of 3 strokes over par on a hole.

Trolley: A two or three-wheeled device used to aid the carrying of a golf bag around the course.

Trouble Shot: A shot taken from a bad lie such as in a bunker or rough.

Turn: The change from front nine to back nine or vice versa.

Underclubbing: Using a club that does not yield the needed distance.

Underspin: Backspin.

Unplayable Lie: A lie from which it is impossible to play the ball such as inside a bush.

Up: A golfer's lead in strokes or holes over an opponent.

Up & Down: Taking two strokes from the current position (usually a rough or bunker) to hole the ball. In other words; one shot to bring the ball up and the next shot to play the ball down the hole.

Uphill Lie: A position of the ball on a slope in which a right-handed golfer's left foot is higher than his right foot.

Upright Swing: A swing in which the club is carried directly backward and upward from the ball.

USGA: United States Golf Association.

Vardon Grip: See 'Overlapping Grip'.

Waggle: A preliminary movement of the clubhead behind and over the ball in preparation to the swing.

Water Hazard: A hazard that contains water.

Water Hole: A hole with water such as a stream or lake that forces the players to play their balls over it.

Wedge: An iron with a heavy flange on the bottom and a high loft.

Whiff: To swing and miss the ball.

Whipping: The thread or twine wrapped around the area where the shaft joins the head. It's often replaced by a plastic ferrule.

Whippy: A very flexible shaft.

Wind Cheater: A shot played low against the wind. It is played with strong backspin, starts low and rises only toward the end of the shot.

Winter Rules: Local rules that allow a golfer to improve the lie of the ball on the fairway.

Wood: Formerly a club with a wooden head. Now the term pertains to a club that has a large head of wood, metal or other material.

Wormburner: A hard hit ball that stays close to the ground.

Wrong Ball: According to the rules, a wrong ball is any ball that is not the layer's ball in play, his provisional ball or his second ball played under the rules.

Yardage Chart: A printed card detailing the layout and yardage of each hole on the course.

Yips: A bout of nerves that make it difficult for a player to putt properly.

Made in the USA
Las Vegas, NV
09 February 2021